NORTH AMERICAN
WETLANDS CONSERVATION ACT
PROGRESS REPORT
2006~2007

NORTH AMERICAN WETLANDS CONSERVATION ACT PROGRESS REPORT 2006~2007

North American Wetlands Conservation Council
March 2008

Table of Contents

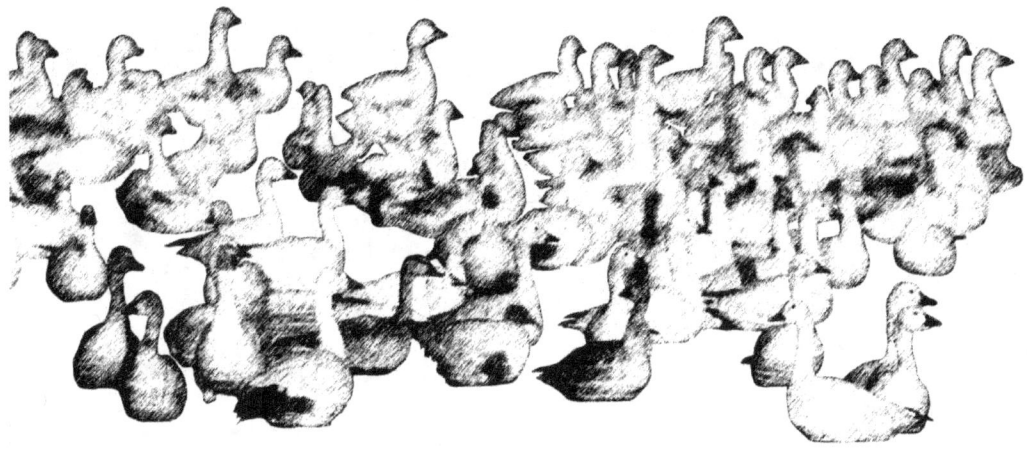

North American Wetlands Conservation Act
Reporting Requirements

This document fulfills the requirements of Section 10 and 16 of the North American Wetlands Conservation Act of 1989.

Sec. 10. REPORT TO CONGRESS.

The Secretary shall report to the appropriate Committees on the implementation of this Act. The report shall include—

(1) a biennial assessment of—

(A) the estimated number of acres of wetlands and habitat for waterfowl and other migratory birds that were restored, protected, or enhanced during such two-year period by Federal, State, and local agencies and other entities in the United States, Canada, and Mexico;

(B) trends in the populations size and distribution of North American migratory birds;

(C) the status of efforts to establish agreements with nations in the western hemisphere pursuant to section 16; and

(D) wetlands conservation projects funded under this Act, listed and identified by type, conservation mechanism (such as acquisition, easement, or lease), location, and duration.

(2) an annual assessment of the status of wetlands conservation projects, including an accounting of expenditures by Federal, State, and other United States entities, and expenditures by Canadian and Mexican sources to carry out these projects.

Sec. 16. OTHER AGREEMENTS.

(a) The Secretary shall undertake with the appropriate officials of nations in the western hemisphere to establish agreements, modeled after the [North American Waterfowl Management] Plan or the [Tripartite] Agreement, for the protection of migratory birds identified in section 13(a)(5) of the Fish and Wildlife Conservation Act of 1980 (16 U.S.C. 2912(a)). When any such agreements are reached, the Secretary shall make recommendations to the appropriate Committees on legislation necessary to implement the agreements.

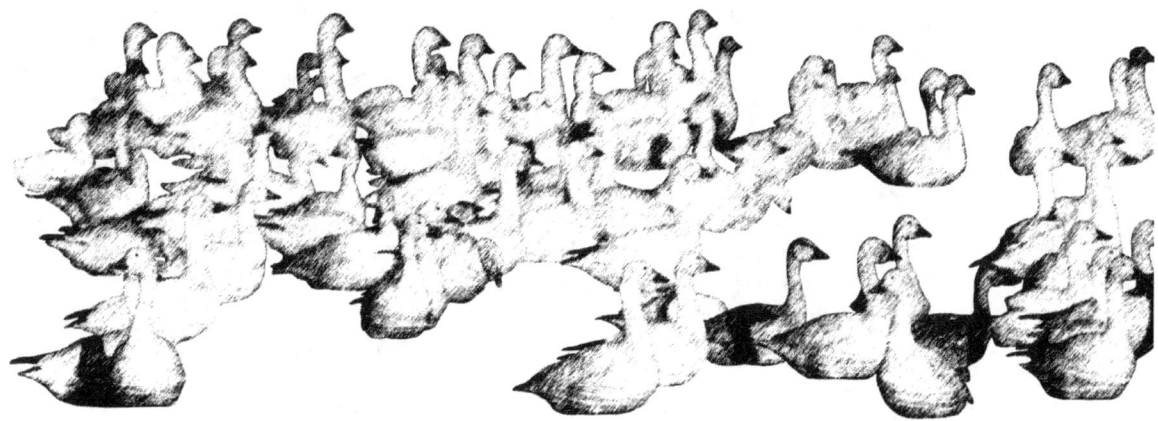

Abbreviations Used in Tables

U.S. States/Territories

AK	Alaska
AL	Alabama
AZ	Arizona
CA	California
CO	Colorado
DE	Delaware
FL	Florida
GA	Georgia
IA	Iowa
ID	Idaho
IL	Illinois
IN	Indiana
KS	Kansas
KY	Kentucky
LA	Louisiana
MA	Massachusetts
ME	Maine
MI	Michigan
MN	Minnesota
MO	Missouri
MT	Montana
NC	North Carolina
ND	North Dakota
NE	Nebraska
NH	New Hampshire
NJ	New Jersey
NM	New Mexico
NY	New York
OH	Ohio
OR	Oregon
PA	Pennsylvania
PR	Puerto Rico
SC	South Carolina
SD	South Dakota
TN	Tennessee
TX	Texas
UT	Utah
VA	Virginia
WA	Washington
WI	Wisconsin
WY	Wyoming

Other

JV	Joint Venture
NWR	National Wildlife Refuge
SRA	State Recreation Area
WMA	Wildlife Management Area

Canadian Provinces

AB	Alberta
BC	British Columbia
MB	Manitoba
NB	New Brunswick
NF	Newfoundland
NS	Nova Scotia
NT	Northwest Territories
ON	Ontario
PEI	Prince Edward Island
QC	Quebec
SK	Saskatchewan
YT	Yukon Territories

Mexican States

AGS	Aguascalientes
BCN	Baja California Norte
BCS	Baja California Sur
CAM	Campeche
CHIS	Chiapas
CHIH	Chihuahua
COAH	Coahuila
COL	Colima
DF	Distrito Federal
DGO	Durango
GRO	Guerrero
GTO	Guanajuato
HGO	Hidalgo
JAL	Jalisco
MEX	Mexico
MICH	Michoacan
MOR	Morelos
NAY	Nayarit
NL	Nuevo Leon
OAX	Oaxaca
PUE	Puebla
QRO	Queretaro
QROO	Quintana Roo
SIN	Sinaloa
SLP	San Luis Potosi
SON	Sonora
TAB	Tabasco
TAMPS	Tamaulipas
TLAX	Tlaxcala
VER	Veracruz
YUC	Yucatan
ZAC	Zacatecas

Project Type

P	Protected
H	Habitat Management (eg., restoration and/or enhancement)
O	Other

2

U.S. North American Wetlands Conservation Act Projects Arrayed by State
Acres Protected, Restored, and Enhanced in Fiscal Years 2006-2007
[Section 10(1)(A)]

Project Title	State/Territory	Protected Acres	Restored Acres	Enhanced Acres	Date Approved
Chena Flats Greenbelt Project	AK	85	0	0	6/21/2005
Chena Flats Greenbelt Project - Ketzler Property	AK	92	0	0	6/14/2006
Potter Marsh State Wildlife Refuge Protection Project	AK	5	0	0	6/21/2005
Total		**181**	**0**	**0**	
Bottomland Conservation in the Arkansas Delta	AR	1,720	682	0	3/8/2006
Lower Mississippi Valley Ecosystem IV	AR, LA, MS	1,400	5,346	10,462	9/13/2006
Private Lands in the Lower Mississippi Valley & Gulf Coastal Plain II	AR, LA, MS	6,698	11,500	7,500	9/21/2005
Total		**9,818**	**17,528**	**17,962**	
Cibola NWR Wetlands Project	AZ	0	80	420	6/13/2007
Sonoran Wetlands Restoration I	AZ, CA	930	433	3,324	3/14/2007
Total		**930**	**513**	**3,744**	
Burton Property - Litchfield Habitat Restoration & Enhancement Project	CA	0	77	0	6/21/2005
Butte & Colusa Basins Wetlands Project	CA	3,329	1,047	17,979	3/14/2007
Coastal Marin Wetlands Restoration Project I	CA	0	754	0	9/13/2006
Elmwood Tract Phase I	CA	0	33	67	6/13/2007
Freshwater Creek Estuary Rehabilitation Project	CA	54	35	0	6/21/2005
Humboldt Bay Coastal Education Center & Reserve	CA	38	0	0	6/13/2007
Janes Creek Log Pond Acquisition Project	CA	7	7	0	6/21/2005
Mad River Slough Coastal Wetland Enhancement & Salt Marsh Restoration	CA	0	3	11	6/13/2007
Modoc Plateau/Pit River Wetlands Project	CA	2,080	1,417	2,444	3/8/2006
North Sacramento Valley Wetland Habitat Project II	CA	0	3,333	3,233	9/21/2005
North San Joaquin Valley Wetland Habitat Project II	CA	881	507	14,916	3/8/2006
Northern Tulare/San Joaquin Basins I	CA	949	314	21,953	9/21/2005
San Dieguito Lepidium Latifolium Control Project	CA	0	130	0	6/13/2007
San Joaquin Basin Wetland Restoration II	CA	0	590	0	6/21/2005
Sonoran Wetlands Restoration I	CA, AZ	930	433	3,324	3/14/2007
South San Francisco Bay Wetlands Restoration Project	CA	0	11,585	1,133	9/13/2006
Yolo Basin Wetland Habitat Project III	CA	0	3,928	0	3/14/2007
Total		**8,268**	**24,193**	**65,060**	
Conservation of a Playa Complex in Eastern Colorado	CO	640	3	637	6/21/2005
Huerfano Lake Conservation & Restoration Project	CO	0	161	320	6/14/2006
Lower South Platte River Wetland & Riparian Restoration II	CO	4,047	2,244	250	9/21/2005
Lower South Platte Wetland Initiative	CO	0	540	0	6/14/2006
San Luis Valley Wetland Project III	CO	12,303	1,120	0	3/8/2006
The Miller Ranch Preservation Project	CO	200	0	125	6/14/2006
Total		**17,190**	**4,068**	**1,332**	
Aton Forest Preservation Project	CT	1,166	0	0	6/14/2006
Total		**1,166**	**0**	**0**	

Multistate projects are listed in each state/territory where they occur. Full figures are given with each listing.

U.S. North American Wetlands Conservation Act Projects Arrayed by State
Acres Protected, Restored, and Enhanced in Fiscal Years 2006-2007
[Section 10(1)(A)]

Project Title	State/ Territory	Protected Acres	Restored Acres	Enhanced Acres	Date Approved
Invasive Species Eradication & Mangrove Planting in the Indian River Lagoon	FL	0	38	0	6/21/2005
Total		**0**	**38**	**0**	
Kauai Wetland Restoration Phase I	HI	18	44	0	6/14/2006
Total		**18**	**44**	**0**	
Cedar - Wapsi Valley Wetlands	IA	2,037	0	0	9/13/2006
Central Iowa Protected Water Areas Wetland Conservation Project	IA	95	0	0	6/14/2006
Iowa Living Lakes - Diamond Lake	IA	0	0	166	6/21/2005
Iowa Prairie Pothole Upland Habitat Development II	IA	0	948	0	6/14/2006
Middle Missouri River II	IA, NE	4,090	627	2,930	3/8/2006
Mitchell County Wetland Habitat Development	IA	82	185	0	6/21/2005
Prairie Lakes Wetland Initiative	IA	2,676	5	405	3/14/2007
Total		**8,980**	**1,765**	**3,501**	
Bear Lake Valley Wetlands Restoration	ID	0	5,514	8,635	9/21/2005
Camas Creek Ranch	ID	0	1,910	0	6/21/2005
Henry's Fork Wetlands II	ID	4,463	1,872	0	9/21/2005
Lower Clark Fork River/Lake Pend Oreille Watershed	ID, MT	2,537	20	617	3/14/2007
Total		**7,000**	**9,316**	**9,252**	
Black Gold Nesting Habitat Enhancement Project	IL	0	36	250	6/21/2005
Burning Star 5 Wetland Enhancement Project	IL	0	175	70	6/14/2006
Michael Wolff Memorial Wetland Project	IL	0	100	0	6/21/2005
Restoring a Large Native Prairie/Wetland Complex	IL	0	164	0	6/21/2005
Total		**0**	**475**	**320**	
Goose Pond Fish & Wildlife Area Moist Soil Enhancement Project	IN	60	0	58	6/13/2007
Limberlost & Loblolly Wetland Restoration Project	IN	228	121	0	6/21/2005
Total		**288**	**121**	**58**	
Frazier Park Lake Restoration Project: Sediment Removal	KS	0	18	10	6/21/2005
Jamestown Wildlife Area Phase I	KS	710	1,510	550	3/8/2006
Total		**710**	**1,528**	**560**	
Three Ponds State Nature Preserve Addition #1: Bottomland Hardwood	KY	315	274	0	6/14/2006
Total		**315**	**274**	**0**	

Multistate projects are listed in each state/territory where they occur. Full figures are given with each listing.

U.S. North American Wetlands Conservation Act Projects Arrayed by State
Acres Protected, Restored, and Enhanced in Fiscal Years 2006-2007
[Section 10(1)(A)]

Project Title	State/ Territory	Protected Acres	Restored Acres	Enhanced Acres	Date Approved
Acadiana Park Wetland Preservation	LA	25	0	0	6/21/2005
Chenier Plain Coastal Wetlands Conservation IV	LA, TX	1,162	640	0	3/8/2006
Chenier Plain Coastal Wetlands Conservation V	LA, TX	1,151	0	0	9/13/2006
Grand Cote NWR Wetland Enhancement	LA	319	0	1,828	3/14/2007
Gulf Coast Wetlands Restoration & Enhancement	LA	0	292	10,732	3/14/2007
Lafitte Terracing Project	LA	0	5,438	0	3/8/2006
Louisiana Coastal Wetlands III	LA	0	2,236	0	9/21/2005
Lower Mississippi Valley Ecosystem IV	LA, AR, MS	1,400	5,346	10,462	9/13/2006
Lower Neches River Cypress	LA, TX	2,950	0	0	3/14/2007
Maurepas/Pontchartrain Habitat Conservation II	LA	7,600	0	0	9/21/2005
Maurepas/Pontchartrain Habitat Conservation III	LA	2,530	0	0	3/14/2007
Private Lands in the Lower Mississippi Valley & Gulf Coastal Plain II	LA, AR, MS	6,698	11,500	7,500	9/21/2005
Sabine Island WMA - Acquisition Effort	LA	600	0	0	3/8/2006
Total		**24,435**	**25,452**	**30,522**	
Buzzards Bay Watershed: Dike Creek	MA	252	15	0	9/13/2006
Buzzards Bay Watershed: Inner Bay Restoration & Edmunds	MA	102	90	0	9/13/2006
Buzzards Bay Watershed: Nasketucket Bay II	MA	176	0	0	9/21/2005
Buzzards Bay Watershed: Slocums River	MA	93	0	0	9/13/2006
Buzzards Bay Watershed: Westport River	MA	207	0	0	9/21/2005
Buzzards Bay Wetlands Project	MA	20	0	0	6/13/2007
Fitzgerald Lake Conservation Area & Saw Mill Hills Conservation Area	MA	100	0	0	6/21/2005
Upper Great Marsh Tidal Marsh Restoration	MA	0	150	0	6/14/2006
Wetland Habitat Restoration at Woodbridge Island	MA	0	23	0	6/13/2007
Total		**950**	**278**	**0**	
Allegheny Mountain - Northern Ridge & Valley	MD, VA, WV	0	434	0	6/13/2007
E.A. Vaughn WMA Wetland Restoration Project	MD	0	400	0	6/21/2005
Pocomoke River Conservation Partnership I	MD	1,188	655	0	9/13/2006
Total		**1,188**	**1,489**	**0**	
Big Hill & Second Pond Forest Reserve	ME	1,609	0	0	6/14/2006
Blaisdell - Clough I on the York River	ME	25	0	0	6/21/2005
Caribou Bog/Katahdin Iron Works	ME	3,070	0	0	6/14/2006
Conserving a Network of Wetlands in the Tatnics: Tatnic Woods III	ME	29	0	0	6/21/2005
Greater Pleasant Bay Project Area II	ME	676	0	0	9/13/2006
Greater York River Project Area	ME	934	0	0	9/21/2005
Kennebec Estuary, Maine Phase II	ME	631	0	0	9/13/2006
Machias River Project	ME	7,785	0	0	9/21/2005
Northeast Penjajawoc Property Acquisition	ME	83	0	0	6/14/2006
Northern Corea Heath Acquisition	ME	606	0	0	6/14/2006
Richardson Seal Cove Property Acquisition	ME	43	0	0	6/21/2005
Sucker Brook Project	ME	227	0	0	6/14/2006
Upper Saco River Project: Hancock I	ME	408	0	0	6/21/2005
Total		**16,126**	**0**	**0**	

Multistate projects are listed in each state/territory where they occur. Full figures are given with each listing.

U.S. North American Wetlands Conservation Act Projects Arrayed by State
Acres Protected, Restored, and Enhanced in Fiscal Years 2006-2007
[Section 10(1)(A)]

Project Title	State/ Territory	Protected Acres	Restored Acres	Enhanced Acres	Date Approved
Gateway To The Jordan River	MI	110	0	0	6/13/2007
Nayanquing Point SWA Coastal Wetland & Grassland	MI	0	0	865	6/21/2005
Saginaw Bay to Lake Erie Coastal Habitat Project	MI	965	1,626	1,330	9/21/2005
Saint Clair Lake/Six Mile Lake Natural Area Addition	MI	51	0	0	6/13/2007
Wetland Property Acquisition for Migratory Birds	MI	82	0	0	6/21/2005
Wigwam Bay SWA Coastal Wetland Restoration	MI	0	135	0	6/14/2006
Total		**1,208**	**1,761**	**2,195**	
Border Prairie Wetlands	MN	1,330	284	818	9/13/2006
Carlos Avery WMA Wetland Enhancements	MN	0	0	625	6/14/2006
Geneva Lake Conservation Easements	MN	250	0	0	6/14/2006
Lower Minnesota Prairie Coteau	MN	65	50	0	6/14/2006
Lower Minnesota Valley Wetland Conservation	MN	834	794	1,255	3/8/2006
Minnesota Headwaters I	MN	808	715	3,596	9/13/2006
Rapids Lake Acquisition & Restoration Project	MN	116	40	0	6/21/2005
Roberts Waterfowl Production Area Restoration	MN	280	280	0	6/21/2005
Upper Minnesota River Valley Phase I	MN	1,554	90	825	3/14/2007
Total		**5,237**	**2,253**	**7,119**	
Lewis & Clark Floodplain Heritage Partnership III	MO	1,183	0	3,004	9/13/2006
Montrose Wetland Restoration Partnership	MO	0	110	0	6/13/2007
Total		**1,183**	**110**	**3,004**	
Lower Mississippi Valley Ecosystem IV	MS, AR, LA	1,400	5,346	10,462	9/13/2006
Malmaison WMA Forested Wetlands Enhancement	MS	1,129	243	1,030	9/13/2006
Private Lands in the Lower Mississippi Valley & Gulf Coastal Plain II	MS, AR, LA	6,698	11,500	7,500	9/21/2005
Total		**9,227**	**17,089**	**18,992**	
Carter Ponds Restoration & Enhancement Project	MT	0	52	0	6/14/2006
Lower Clark Fork River/Lake Pend Oreille Watershed	MT, ID	2,537	20	617	3/14/2007
Madison/Gallatin Wetlands Conservation Project I	MT	5,867	88	0	3/8/2006
Madison/Gallatin Wetlands Conservation Project II	MT	2,958	57	0	3/14/2007
The Bitterroot Wetland Conservation Corridor	MT	0	343	228	6/14/2006
Total		**11,362**	**560**	**845**	
Butner - Falls of Neuse Game Land Managed Wetlands Enhancement Project	NC	0	0	246	6/21/2005
Invasive Species Eradication & Habitat Revitalization: Orton Plantation	NC	0	188	0	6/13/2007
North Carolina Onslow Bight Partnership II	NC	10,425	1,619	0	9/21/2005
Roanoke River Migratory Bird Initiative II	NC, VA	532	1,204	700	3/8/2006
Sound Investment Phase II	NC, VA	3,458	0	969	9/21/2005
Suggs Millpond Game Land Managed Wetlands Enhancement Project	NC	53	0	130	6/21/2005
Total		**14,468**	**3,011**	**2,045**	

Multistate projects are listed in each state/territory where they occur. Full figures are given with each listing.

U.S. North American Wetlands Conservation Act Projects Arrayed by State
Acres Protected, Restored, and Enhanced in Fiscal Years 2006-2007
[Section 10(1)(A)]

Project Title	State/ Territory	Protected Acres	Restored Acres	Enhanced Acres	Date Approved
Chase Lake Area Wetland Project VII	ND	31,197	284	11,776	9/13/2006
Missouri Coteau Habitat Conservation Project IV	ND	18,445	0	0	9/21/2005
Missouri Coteau Habitat Conservation Project V	ND	21,415	0	0	9/13/2006
Mouse River Watershed Enhancement Project V	ND	17,293	684	5,964	3/8/2006
North Dakota Drift Prairie Project I	ND	20,585	639	2,678	9/13/2006
North Dakota Great Plains Project V	ND	17,957	486	831	3/14/2007
Northern Coteau Project V	ND	20,639	490	9,388	9/21/2005
Total		**147,531**	**2,583**	**30,637**	
Big Bend Reach of the Platte River Phase I	NE	1,290	1,027	1,741	3/14/2007
Middle Missouri River II	NE, IA	4,090	627	2,930	3/8/2006
Rainwater Basin Habitat Conservation Project II	NE	825	1,328	8,127	3/14/2007
Total		**6,205**	**2,982**	**12,798**	
Great Bay Estuary VI: Piscassic River Watershed	NH	664	0	0	3/14/2007
Piscassic Greenway Conservation Initiative	NH	329	0	0	6/21/2005
Robb Reservoir Landscape Conservation Project	NH	1,670	0	0	6/14/2006
Wapack Wilderness Conservation Campaign	NH	1,400	0	0	6/13/2007
Total		**4,063**	**0**	**0**	
Ruby Lake NWR Wetland Enhancement	NV	0	0	9,055	6/21/2005
Total		**0**	**0**	**9,055**	
Acquisition & Protection of Private Property within Wetland Complex	NY	15	15	0	6/21/2005
Saint Lawrence River Valley I	NY	4,220	1,839	0	9/21/2005
Total		**4,235**	**1,854**	**0**	
Abraham Marsh Wetland Enhancement Project	OH	0	0	400	6/14/2006
Ohio Grand River Wetlands Project	OH	1,641	131	6	9/21/2005
Total		**1,641**	**131**	**406**	
Shaffer Playa, Oklahoma	OK	212	0	0	6/14/2006
Total		**212**	**0**	**0**	
Lake County Closed Basin Project II	OR	0	2,520	5,045	9/13/2006
Lower Columbia River Ecoregion IV	OR, WA	1,098	31	150	3/8/2006
Lower Columbia River Estuary Project II	OR, WA	436	798	140	9/21/2005
Lower Yaquina Salt Marsh Conservation Project	OR	76	0	0	6/14/2006
Restoration & Enhancement at Oaks Bottom Wildlife Refuge Phase I	OR	0	15	0	6/13/2007
Upper Klamath Lakes Wetlands	OR	5,345	4,508	2,155	9/13/2006
Upper Willamette Wetlands Conservation Initiative II	OR	1,271	1,707	94	3/14/2007
Willamette River Delta Restoration Phase I	OR	369	717	520	3/14/2007
Total		**8,595**	**10,296**	**8,104**	
Buzzards Bay Watershed: Tiverton Great Swamp	RI	230	0	0	9/13/2006
Wetland Restoration on Three NWR & Adjacent Land	RI	0	52	0	6/21/2005
Total		**230**	**52**	**0**	

Multistate projects are listed in each state/territory where they occur. Full figures are given with each listing.

U.S. North American Wetlands Conservation Act Projects Arrayed by State
Acres Protected, Restored, and Enhanced in Fiscal Years 2006-2007
[Section 10(1)(A)]

Project Title	State/ Territory	Protected Acres	Restored Acres	Enhanced Acres	Date Approved
Ace Basin: Edisto River Corridor Protection Project II	SC	4,401	0	0	9/21/2005
Bear Island Club, Inc. Wetlands Restoration Project	SC	0	200	70	6/13/2007
Cedar Island Enhancement Project	SC	0	0	2,316	6/21/2005
Combahee Fields Revitalization Project	SC	0	0	375	6/21/2005
Murphy Island Enhancement Project	SC	0	0	2,572	6/21/2005
Santee NWR Cuddo Unit Project	SC	0	0	900	6/14/2006
South Carolina Pee Dee River Conservation Initiative: Woodbury Tract	SC	25,668	0	0	9/13/2006
South Carolina Savannah River Conservation Initiative: Hamilton Ridge Tract	SC	13,281	0	0	9/13/2006
Total		**43,350**	**200**	**6,233**	
James River Lowlands/Missouri Coteau Project II	SD	8,426	0	0	3/8/2006
James River Lowlands/Missouri Coteau Project III	SD	6,081	0	0	3/14/2007
Total		**14,507**	**0**	**0**	
Big Swan Headwaters Preserve: Boiling Springs Tract	TN	27	11	0	6/13/2007
Lower Obion River III	TN	1,325	982	75	3/8/2006
Restoration of Lick Creek Wetlands - Joachim Bible Refuge Tracts	TN	273	276	0	6/14/2006
Wolf River, Tennessee Phase II	TN	2,411	0	2,100	3/14/2007
Total		**4,036**	**1,269**	**2,175**	
Austins Woods III	TX	877	0	0	3/14/2007
Chenier Plain Coastal Wetlands Conservation IV	TX, LA	1,162	640	0	3/8/2006
Chenier Plain Coastal Wetlands Conservation V	TX, LA	1,151	0	0	9/13/2006
Coastal Prairie Wetlands Restoration & Acquisition	TX	6,978	3,390	0	9/21/2005
Gulf Coast JV Mottled Duck Conservation Plan	TX	160	250	0	6/13/2007
Lower Neches River Cypress	TX, LA	2,950	0	0	3/14/2007
Mud Flats Pass Culvert Project	TX	0	219	0	6/14/2006
Rio Bosque Water Supply Well	TX	0	68	0	6/21/2005
Wetland Enhancement for the Myrtle Foester - Whitmire Preserve	TX	0	0	1,140	6/21/2005
Wetland Restoration & Enhancement of Private & Public Lands of the Texas Gulf Coast V	TX	0	11,843	2,665	3/14/2007
Total		**13,278**	**16,410**	**3,805**	
The New State Wetland Enhancement	UT	0	0	1,200	6/21/2005
Total		**0**	**0**	**1,200**	
Allegheny Mountain - Northern Ridge & Valley	VA, WV, MD	0	434	0	6/13/2007
Lower Rappahannock Phase III	VA	3,497	0	0	3/8/2006
Roanoke River Migratory Bird Initiative II	VA, NC	532	1,204	700	3/8/2006
Sound Investment Phase II	VA, NC	3,458	0	969	9/21/2005
Southern Tip Cooperative Conservation Initiative	VA	1,872	145	233	9/13/2006
Total		**9,359**	**1,783**	**1,902**	

Multistate projects are listed in each state/territory where they occur. Full figures are given with each listing.

U.S. North American Wetlands Conservation Act Projects Arrayed by State
Acres Protected, Restored, and Enhanced in Fiscal Years 2006-2007
[Section 10(1)(A)]

Project Title	State/ Territory	Protected Acres	Restored Acres	Enhanced Acres	Date Approved
Bagley Lake Farm Wetland Restoration, Olympic Peninsula	WA	0	10	0	6/21/2005
Chehalis River Floodplain & Estuary Wetland Conservation	WA	2,962	1,006	0	3/8/2006
Crow Marsh Project - Crow Marsh East	WA	14	0	0	6/13/2007
Lower Columbia River Ecoregion IV	WA, OR	1,098	31	150	3/8/2006
Lower Columbia River Estuary Project II	WA, OR	436	798	140	9/21/2005
Lower Yakima Wetlands Protection/Restoration II	WA	320	14,539	679	9/13/2006
Lummi Island Conservation Project	WA	436	0	0	6/14/2006
Middle Puget Sound Wetlands Phase I	WA	187	370	12	9/21/2005
North Willapa Bay Wetlands Conservation	WA	1,391	875	0	9/13/2006
Otto Preserve Expansion Project	WA	24	0	0	6/21/2005
Total		**6,868**	**17,629**	**981**	
Hawk Metals Wetland Acquisition	WI	720	0	0	6/14/2006
Leopold Memorial Reserve - Migratory Habitat Expansion	WI	15	0	0	6/21/2005
Lower Chippewa River Wetland Protection Partnership II	WI	2,636	175	0	3/8/2006
Scuppernong River Wetland Restoration Phase II	WI	0	200	0	6/21/2005
Southcentral Wisconsin Prairie Pothole Initiative III	WI	2,908	886	490	9/21/2005
The Des Plaines River Lowlands Conservation Project	WI	38	38	0	6/13/2007
Whitefish Lake & Wetland Preservation	WI	37	0	0	6/21/2005
Willow River & Kinnickinnic State Parks Nesting Habitat Enhancement	WI	0	305	438	6/21/2005
Wisconsin Private Lands Conservation: 10 Projects in Southern Wisconsin	WI	0	89	0	6/21/2005
Total		**6,354**	**1,693**	**928**	
Allegheny Mountain - Northern Ridge & Valley	WV, MD, VA	0	434	0	6/13/2007
Total		**0**	**434**	**0**	

Multistate projects are listed in each state/territory where they occur. Full figures are given with each listing.

Canadian North American Wetlands Conservation Act Projects Arrayed by Province
Acres Protected, Restored, and Enhanced in Fiscal Years 2006-2007
[Section 10(1)(A)]

Project Title	Province/ Territory	Protected Acres	Restored Acres	Enhanced Acres	Date Approved
Alberta Habitat Program	AB, BC	1,174	0	1,708	9/21/2005
Canadian Intermountain JV & Pacific Coast JV Wetland - Associated Migratory Bird Habitat	AB, BC	345	0	169	9/21/2005
Canadian Intermountain JV & Pacific Coast JV Wetland - Associated Migratory Bird Habitat	AB, BC	181	0	154	6/14/2006
Canadian Intermountain JV & Pacific Coast JV Wetland - Associated Migratory Bird Habitat	AB, BC	179	0	150	6/13/2007
Critical Wetland & Upland Habitat - Alberta	AB	4,500	0	8,320	9/21/2005
Potholes Plus Project	AB, MB	5,600	0	200	9/21/2005
Potholes Plus Project	AB, MB, SK	6,680	0	320	6/13/2007
Prairie - Western Boreal Region Habitat Program	AB, BC, MB, NT, SK, YT	61,956	0	26,462	6/14/2006
Prairie - Western Boreal Region Habitat Program	AB, BC, MB, NT, SK, YT	20,280	0	8,662	9/13/2006
Prairie - Western Boreal Region Habitat Program	AB, BC, MB, NT, SK, YT	57,406	0	49,048	6/13/2007
Prairie Canada Wetlands & Uplands	AB, SK	14,800	0	3,600	6/14/2006
Prairie Canada Wetlands & Uplands	AB, MB, SK	13,900	0	3,620	6/13/2007
Total		**171,927**	**0**	**97,085**	
Alberta Habitat Program	BC, AB	1,174	0	1,708	9/21/2005
Canadian Intermountain JV & Pacific Coast JV Wetland - Associated Migratory Bird Habitat	BC, AB	345	0	169	9/21/2005
Canadian Intermountain JV & Pacific Coast JV Wetland - Associated Migratory Bird Habitat	BC, AB	181	0	154	6/14/2006
Canadian Intermountain JV & Pacific Coast JV Wetland - Associated Migratory Bird Habitat	BC, AB	179	0	150	6/13/2007
Critical Wetlands & Associated Upland Habitats	BC	853	0	690	9/21/2005
Critical Wetlands & Associated Upland Habitats	BC	1,420	0	1,975	6/14/2006
Critical Wetlands & Associated Upland Habitats	BC	490	0	2,550	9/13/2006
Critical Wetlands & Associated Upland Habitats	BC	935	0	3,250	6/13/2007
Prairie - Western Boreal Region Habitat Program	BC, AB, MB, NT, SK, YT	61,956	0	26,462	6/14/2006
Prairie - Western Boreal Region Habitat Program	BC, AB, MB, NT, SK, YT	20,280	0	8,662	9/13/2006
Prairie - Western Boreal Region Habitat Program	BC, AB, MB, NT, SK, YT	57,406	0	49,048	6/13/2007
Total	**1**	**45,219**	**0**	**94,818**	
Manitoba Critical Wetland & Upland Habitat	MB	2,240	0	520	9/21/2005
Potholes Plus Project	MB, AB	5,600	0	200	9/21/2005
Potholes Plus Project	MB, AB, SK	6,680	0	320	6/13/2007
Prairie - Western Boreal Region Habitat Program	MB, BC, AB, NT, SK, YT	61,956	0	26,462	6/14/2006
Prairie - Western Boreal Region Habitat Program	MB, BC, AB, NT, SK, YT	20,280	0	8,662	9/13/2006
Prairie - Western Boreal Region Habitat Program	MB, BC, AB, NT, SK, YT	57,406	0	49,048	6/13/2007
Prairie Canada Wetlands & Uplands	MB, AB, SK	13,900	0	3,620	6/13/2007
Total		**168,062**	**0**	**88,832**	

Multistate projects are listed in each provice/territory where they occur. Full figures are given with each listing.

Canadian North American Wetlands Conservation Act Projects Arrayed by Province
Acres Protected, Restored, and Enhanced in Fiscal Years 2006-2007
[Section 10(1)(A)]

Project Title	Province/ Territory	Protected Acres	Restored Acres	Enhanced Acres	Date Approved
Atlantic Canada Wetland Securement Project	NB, NF	200	0	0	9/21/2005
Atlantic Canada Wetlands Conservation	NB, NF, NS	1,479	0	159	9/21/2005
Atlantic Coastal Waterfowl Habitat Conservation	NB, PE	1,500	0	0	6/13/2007
Eastern Habitat JV Wetlands Conservation	NB, NF, NS, ON, PE, QC	6,973	0	2,808	6/14/2006
Eastern Habitat JV Wetlands Conservation	NB, NF, NS, ON, PE, QC	3,057	0	833	9/13/2006
Eastern Habitat JV Wetlands Conservation	NB, NF, NS, ON, PE, QC	3,410	0	2,532	6/13/2007
Maritimes Wetland Securement Project	NB, NS, PE	500	0	0	6/14/2006
Total		**17,119**	**0**	**6,332**	
Atlantic Canada Wetland Securement Project	NF, NB	200	0	0	9/21/2005
Atlantic Canada Wetlands Conservation	NF, NB, NS	1,479	0	159	9/21/2005
Eastern Habitat JV Wetlands Conservation	NF, NB, NS, ON, PE, QC	6,973	0	2,808	6/14/2006
Eastern Habitat JV Wetlands Conservation	NF, NB, NS, ON, PE, QC	3,057	0	833	9/13/2006
Eastern Habitat JV Wetlands Conservation	NF, NB, NS, ON, PE, QC	3,410	0	2,532	6/13/2007
Total		**15,119**	**0**	**6,332**	
Atlantic Canada Wetlands Conservation	NS, NB, NF	1,479	0	159	9/21/2005
Eastern Habitat JV Wetlands Conservation	NS, NB, NF, ON, PE, QC	6,973	0	2,808	6/14/2006
Eastern Habitat JV Wetlands Conservation	NS, NB, NF, ON, PE, QC	3,057	0	833	9/13/2006
Eastern Habitat JV Wetlands Conservation	NS, NB, NF, ON, PE, QC	3,410	0	2,532	6/13/2007
Maritimes Wetland Securement Project	NS, NB, PE	500	0	0	6/14/2006
Total		**15,419**	**0**	**6,332**	
Prairie - Western Boreal Region Habitat Program	NT, AB, BC, MB, SK, YT	61,956	0	26,462	6/14/2006
Prairie - Western Boreal Region Habitat Program	NT, AB, BC, MB, SK, YT	20,280	0	8,662	9/13/2006
Prairie - Western Boreal Region Habitat Program	NT, AB, BC, MB, SK, YT	57,406	0	49,048	6/13/2007
Total		**139,642**	**0**	**84,172**	
Ducks Unlimited Canada Ontario Project	ON	282	0	197	9/21/2005
Eastern Habitat JV Wetlands Conservation	ON, NB, NF, NS, PE, QC	6,973	0	2,808	6/14/2006
Eastern Habitat JV Wetlands Conservation	ON, NB, NF, NS, PE, QC	3,057	0	833	9/13/2006
Eastern Habitat JV Wetlands Conservation	ON, NB, NF, NS, PE, QC	3,410	0	2,532	6/13/2007
Great Lakes Wetlands Habitat Conservation Project	ON	100	0	29	9/21/2005
Ontario Wetland Habitat Fund Program	ON	4,319	0	4,319	9/21/2005
Total		**18,141**	**0**	**10,718**	

Multistate projects are listed in each provice/territory where they occur. Full figures are given with each listing.

11

Canadian North American Wetlands Conservation Act Projects Arrayed by Province
Acres Protected, Restored, and Enhanced in Fiscal Years 2006-2007
[Section 10(1)(A)]

Project Title	Province/ Territory	Protected Acres	Restored Acres	Enhanced Acres	Date Approved
Atlantic Coastal Waterfowl Habitat Conservation	PE, NB	1,500	0	0	6/13/2007
Eastern Habitat JV Wetlands Conservation	PE, NB, NF, NS, ON, QC	6,973	0	2,808	6/14/2006
Eastern Habitat JV Wetlands Conservation	PE, NB, NF, NS, ON, QC	3,057	0	833	9/13/2006
Eastern Habitat JV Wetlands Conservation	PE, NB, NF,C NS, ON, QC	3,410	0	2,532	6/13/2007
Maritimes Wetland Securement Project	PE, NB, NS	500	0	0	6/14/2006
Total		**15,440**	**0**	**6,173**	
Eastern Habitat JV Wetlands Conservation	QC, NB, NF, NS, ON, PE	6,973	0	2,808	6/14/2006
Eastern Habitat JV Wetlands Conservation	QC, NB, NF, NS, ON, PE	3,057	0	833	9/13/2006
Eastern Habitat JV Wetlands Conservation	QC, NB, NF, NS, ON, PE	3,410	0	2,532	6/13/2007
Quebec: Protecting Wetland & Upland Habitat	QC	1,311	0	75	6/14/2006
Quebec: Protecting Wetland & Upland Habitat	QC	314	0	43	9/13/2006
Quebec: Protecting Wetland & Upland Habitat	QC	860	0	0	6/13/2007
Quebec/Saint Lawrence Watershed	QC	750	0	422	9/21/2005
Saint Lawrence River & Lake Champlain Critical Wetland Habitat Project	QC	200	0	200	9/21/2005
Total		**16,875**	**0**	**6,913**	
Potholes Plus Project	SK, AB, MB	6,680	0	320	6/13/2007
Prairie - Western Boreal Region Habitat Program	SK, AB, BC, MB, NT, YT	61,956	0	26,462	6/14/2006
Prairie - Western Boreal Region Habitat Program	SK, AB, BC, MB, NT, YT	20,280	0	8,662	9/13/2006
Prairie - Western Boreal Region Habitat Program	SK, AB, BC, MB, NT, YT	57,406	0	49,048	6/13/2007
Prairie Canada Wetlands & Uplands	SK, AB	14,800	0	3,600	6/14/2006
Prairie Canada Wetlands & Uplands	SK, AB, MB	13,900	0	3,620	6/13/2007
Saskatchewan Habitat Program	SK	2,192	0	2,019	9/21/2005
Saskatchewan Wetlands & Uplands	SK	4,000	0	250	9/21/2005
Total		**181,214**	**0**	**93,981**	
Prairie - Western Boreal Region Habitat Program	YT, AB, BC, MB, NT, SK	61,956	0	26,462	6/14/2006
Prairie - Western Boreal Region Habitat Program	YT, AB, BC, MB, NT, SK	20,280	0	8,662	9/13/2006
Prairie - Western Boreal Region Habitat Program	YT, AB, BC, MB, NT, SK	57,406	0	49,048	6/13/2007
Total		**139,642**	**0**	**84,172**	

Multistate projects are listed in each provice/territory where they occur. Full figures are given with each listing.

Mexican North American Wetlands Conservation Act Projects Arrayed by State
Acres Protected, Restored, and Enhanced in Fiscal Years 2006-2007
[Section 10(1)(A)]

Project Title	State	Protected Acres	Restored Acres	Enhanced Acres	Date Approved
Joint Initiative for the Restoration of the Colorado River Delta	BCN, SON	0	4,200	0	3/8/2006
Total		**0**	**4,200**	**0**	
Implementation of Legal Conservation Mechanisms in Laguna San Ignacio II	BCS	6,669	0	0	3/14/2007
Total		**6,669**	**0**	**0**	
Waterfowl Reserve Network in Northwest Chihuahua	CHIH	7,413	1,235	0	3/8/2006
Total		**7,413**	**1,235**	**0**	
Protection, Management & Rehabilation of Lajoya - Buenavista & Manguito - Chocohuital Wetlands	CHIS	2,965	49,663	32,908	3/14/2007
Total		**2,965**	**49,663**	**32,908**	
Waterfowl Refuges in Cuatrocienegas, Coahuila	COAH	11,119	10,428	0	3/8/2006
Total		**11,119**	**10,428**	**0**	
Wetland Restoration & Public Outreach Program for the Conservation of the Malaga Wetlands	DGO	0	194	0	3/14/2007
Total		**0**	**194**	**0**	
Ecotourism & Restoration of Habitat at Laguna Sayula II	JAL	0	494	0	3/8/2006
Total		**0**	**494**	**0**	
Conservation of Wintering Areas for Migratory Waterfowl & Shorebirds in Sonora & Sinaloa	SIN, SON	124	0	0	3/14/2007
Restoration Program for Critical Wetland Habitat in Ensenada De Pabellones II	SIN	0	870	0	3/8/2006
Total		**124**	**870**	**0**	
Conservation of Wintering Areas for Migratory Waterfowl & Shorebirds in Sonora & Sinaloa	SON, SIN	124	0	0	3/14/2007
Joint Initiative for the Restoration of the Colorado River Delta	SON, BCN	0	4,200	0	3/8/2006
Total		**124**	**4,200**	**0**	
Lagoon Restoration in the Natural Protected Area of Laguna Madre	TAMPS	0	1,976	0	3/8/2006
Protection of Sea Grasses for the Conservation of Waterfowl in Laguna Madre	TAMPS	86,765	0	0	3/14/2007
Restoration of Wetlands & Land Purchase in the Rio Grande Delta	TAMPS	5,846	4,767	0	3/14/2007
Total		**92,611**	**6,743**	**0**	

Multistate projects are listed in each state where they occur. Full figures are given with each listing.

13

Migratory Bird Trends
[Section 10(1)(B)]

Each year, the U.S. Fish and Wildlife Service, in conjunction with the States, the Canadian Wildlife Service, provincial governments, and other partners, conducts breeding-ground surveys to estimate the size of duck breeding populations. Specialized surveys track trends in the populations of other harvested migratory species such as the mourning dove and the American woodcock. The North American Breeding Bird Survey, conducted annually on approximately 2,900 routes in the United States and Canada by thousands of volunteers, is used to follow changes in the distribution and abundance of many other migratory bird species utilizing wetlands and associated habitats.

Habitat conditions at the time of the breeding waterfowl surveys in May of 2006 and 2007 were generally improved over 2004 and 2005. Wetland conditions in the U.S. portion of the important duck breeding area known as the Prairie Pothole Region were good following a sustained period of dry conditions due to abundant precipitation that began just after 2005 May surveys; however, high quality duck habitat in the Missouri Coteau region remained poor due to continued drought. Alaska's conditions were generally good due to a normal spring ice breakup and good water conditions in abundant beaver ponds and small lakes. Maine also continues to have generally good to excellent conditions, and habitat conditions in western Ontario were excellent over most of the surveyed area. Wetland conditions within the traditional surveyed portion Canada were variable ranging from poor to excellent. Good to excellent conditions occurred in the Canadian Parklands and the western Northwest Territories, while conditions in the southern Saskatchewan and Manitoba remained dry. Southern Alberta improved in 2006 and 2007 due to heavy snowpacks and wet soil conditions.

The total number of ducks surveyed in 2007 was 41.2 million in the traditional survey area, about 24 percent above the long-term average (LTA) of 33.3 million. Seven of the 10 most common duck species exceeded species-specific North American Waterfowl Management Plan (Plan) goals: mallard, gadwall, green-winged teal, blue-winged/cinnamon teal, northern shoveler, redhead, and canvasback. Northern pintail and scaup populations are below Plan objectives. Northern pintail and scaup populations remain depressed and concern lingers about the status of these species. The greater and lesser scaup population estimate was 45 percent below the Plan objective and 33 percent below their LTA. Pintail population estimates were 40 percent below the Plan population goal in 2007 and 19 percent below their LTA.

In the eastern survey area, mallards were 11 percent above their LTA. American black ducks (22 percent) and ring-necked ducks (27 percent) were above their long-term averages. Merganser and goldeneye populations each increased between 2006 and 2007 but were similar to their LTA Eastern populations of scoters, scaup, American wigeon, buffleheads and green-winged teal were populations were similar in 2006 and 2007 and similar to their LTA.

Most goose and swan populations in North America continue to thrive. The following populations displayed significant positive trends over the most recent 10-year period: Mississippi Flyway Giant, Atlantic and Aleutian Canada geese, western Arctic/Wrangle Island snow geese, and Pacific white-fronted geese. Only the eastern population of tundra swans experienced a significant negative 10-year trend.

The dusky Canada goose population remains a concern. Surveys have been changed from wintering ground mark-resight methods to direct breeding ground counts and recent results are not comparable to long-term data. Aleutian Canada geese (listed as endangered in 1967) have increased an average of 14 percent per year during the last 10 winter surveys and are presently above Plan objectives. Recent declines in indices of Mid-continent white-fronted geese resulted in more conservative harvest strategies. The population has declined at an average rate of 5 percent per year, 1997-2006. Overabundant goose populations (i.e., several populations of temperate-nesting Canada geese, greater and lesser snow geese, and Ross's geese) continue to impact habitats and human interests. Harvest strategies to reduce the abundance of these populations have been implemented. While these strategies have reduced the populations' rate of growth, some populations may still be increasing. Additional monitoring data is required to determine if these populations can be held in check through the regulatory options pursued thus far. In 2008 the Service is expected to issue a conservation order for the first time for greater snow geese in the Atlantic Flyway.

Between 2006 and 2007, call-count indices of mourning dove populations (doves heard) continued to increase significantly in the Eastern Management Unit; but did not change significantly in the Central or Western Units. Breeding dove population indices in 2007 increased from 2006 in the 19 combined hunting states (7.1 percent) in the Eastern Unit but not in the combined non-hunting states. Over the past 10 years, no significant trend was indicated for doves heard in either the Eastern or Western Management Unit, whereas the Central Unit showed a significant decline. Over this same period no unit showed a significant trend in doves seen on survey routes. Over the entire 42-year survey period, all three units have exhibited significant declines in mourning doves heard and a significant decline in doves seen in the Western Unit.

Breeding population indices derived through the American Woodcock Singing-ground Survey in 2007 declined 11.6 percent from 2006 in the Eastern Region; however, the Central Region was unchanged. There was not a significant trend in woodcock heard on the survey in either the Eastern or Central Region between 1997 and 2007. This represents the fourth consecutive year since 1992 that the 10-year trend estimate for either region was not a significant decline. There were significant long-term declines in both regions, however, over the period of 1968 to 2007. The 2006 recruitment index was 11 percent higher than the 21005 index and 2 percent higher than the long-term average; however, if current trends in land-use practices persist, continued long-term population declines are likely.

Trends of other migratory bird species vary widely. Of all species groups, grassland nesting birds have exhibited the most consistent negative population trends since the late 1960s, with 64 percent of these species showing significant population declines and 7 percent with significant increasing trends. These patterns can be explained by extensive loss or degradation of grassland habitat from agricultural uses as well as by increases in haying. Restoration of native grasses or planting of dense-nesting cover under the North American Waterfowl Management Plan and funded through the North American Wetlands Conservation Act has produced positive impacts on the density of nesting birds and nest success in the Prairie Pothole Region. These and other critical programs, such as the Conservation Reserve Program and Partners in Flight, provide hope for these beleaguered populations.

As a whole, 34 percent of wetland/open-water-dependent migratory bird species show significant increasing long-term population trends. Fifteen percent of these species exhibit significant declining long-term trends. However, data from the North American Breeding Bird Survey are poor for many of these species, and conclusions must be viewed with caution.

Throughout North America, there are significant decreasing population trends for 36 percent of species breeding in successional or scrub habitats while 30 percent of species breeding in woodland habitats show significant increasing population trends from 1966. However, there are still 30 species that breed in woodland habitats exhibiting significant decreasing population trends over the 41-year period. Population trends for 40 percent of species breeding in urban habitats are significantly declining over the long term, while 20 percent of urban-nesting species are significantly increasing across North America.

The above species groups contain short-distance migrants and neotropical migrants. Short-distance migrants breed and winter north of the United States-Mexico border, while neotropical migrants winter south of it. In certain areas where the number of short-distance migrant species is highest, such as the northeast United States, Great Lakes states, and the Canadian prairie, negative population trends predominate for this group. In all, 37 percent of these species exhibit significant decreasing trends. Regional population trends of neotropical migrants are complex and patterns are difficult to discern. Thirty-four percent of neotropical migrant species have exhibited significant negative population trends since the late 1960s.

For many species, the extent to which population trend is driven by the destruction and degradation of wintering habitats south of the United States is unknown. However, it is believed that habitat loss south of the United States border is contributing to the decline of some of these species.

International cooperation is needed to assure the conservation of habitats used by migratory birds throughout their annual cycles. Continental programs such as the North American Waterfowl Management Plan and North American Wetlands Conservation Act Grants Program foster international cooperation.

International Agreements
[Section 10(1)(C)]

No progress has been made to establish agreements with officials of other nations in the Western Hemisphere for the protection of migratory birds.

U.S. North American Wetlands Conservation Act Projects Arrayed by State
Conservation Mechanisms in Fiscal Years 2006-2007
[Section 10(1)(D)]

Project Title	State	Project Type	Conservation Mechanisms	Acres	Years Duration	Date Approved
Chena Flats Greenbelt Project	AK	P	fee title	85	permanent	6/21/2005
Chena Flats Greenbelt Project - Ketzler Property	AK	P	fee title	92	permanent	6/14/2006
Potter Marsh State Wildlife Refuge Protection Project	AK	P	fee title	5	permanent	6/21/2005
Bottomland Conservation in the Arkansas Delta	AR	P, H	fee title	682	permanent	3/8/2006
			easement	1,038	permanent	
Lower Mississippi Valley Ecosystem IV	AR, LA, MS	P, H, O	easement	1,400	permanent	9/13/2006
Private Lands in the Lower Mississippi Valley & Gulf Coastal Plain II	AR, LA, MS	P, H	easement	6,698	permanent	9/21/2005
Sonoran Wetlands Restoration I	AZ, CA	P, H, O	fee title	930	permanent	3/14/2007
Butte & Colusa Basins Wetlands Project	CA	P, H, O	easement	3,329	permanent	3/14/2007
Freshwater Creek Estuary Rehabilitation Project	CA	P, H, O	fee title	54	permanent	6/21/2005
Humboldt Bay Coastal Education Center & Reserve	CA	P, O	fee title	38	permanent	6/13/2007
Janes Creek Log Pond Acquisition Project	CA	P, H	fee title	7	permanent	6/21/2005
Modoc Plateau/Pit River Wetlands Project	CA	P, H, O	fee title	2,080	permanent	3/8/2006
North San Joaquin Valley Wetland Habitat Project II	CA	P, H, O	fee title	120	permanent	3/8/2006
			easement	761	permanent	
Northern Tulare/ an Joaquin Basins I	CA	P, H, O	easement	949	permanent	9/21/2005
Sonoran Wetlands Restoration I	CA, AZ	P, H, O	fee title	930	permanent	3/14/2007
Conservation of a Playa Complex in Eastern Colorado	CO	P, H, O	agreements	640	10	6/21/2005
Lower South Platte River Wetland & Riparian Restoration II	CO	P, H, O	easement	4,047	permanent	9/21/2005
San Luis Valley Wetland Project III	CO	P, H, O	easement	12,303	permanent	3/8/2006
The Miller Ranch Preservation Project	CO	P, H	easement	200	permanent	6/14/2006
Aton Forest Preservation Project	CT	P	fee title	69	permanent	6/14/2006
			easement	1,097	permanent	
Kauai Wetland Restoration Phase I	HI	P, H	easement	18	permanent	6/14/2006
Cedar - Wapsi Valley Wetlands	IA	P	fee title	2,037	permanent	9/13/2006
Central Iowa Protected Water Areas Wetland Conservation Project	IA	P	fee title	95	permanent	6/14/2006
Middle Missouri River II	IA, NE	P, H, O	fee title	4,090	permanent	3/8/2006
Mitchell County Wetland Habitat Development	IA	P, H	fee title	82	permanent	6/21/2005
Prairie Lakes Wetland Initiative	IA	P, H, O	fee title	2,676	permanent	3/14/2007
Henry's Fork Wetlands II	ID	P, H	easement	4,463	permanent	9/21/2005
Lower Clark Fork River/Lake Pend Oreille Watershed	ID, MT	P, H, O	fee title	1,294	permanent	3/14/2007
			easement	1,243	permanent	
Goose Pond Fish & Wildlife Area Moist Soil Enhancement Project	IN	P, H, O	fee title	60	permanent	6/13/2007
Limberlost & Loblolly Wetland Restoration Project	IN	P, H, O	fee title	228	permanent	6/21/2005
Jamestown Wildlife Area Phase I	KS	P, H, O	fee title	710	permanent	3/8/2006

Multistate projects are listed in each state where they occur. Full figures are given with each listing.

17

U.S. North American Wetlands Conservation Act Projects Arrayed by State
Conservation Mechanisms in Fiscal Years 2006-2007
[Section 10(1)(D)]

Project Title	State	Project Type	Conservation Mechanisms	Acres	Years Duration	Date Approved
Three Ponds State Nature Preserve Addition #1: Bottomland Hardwood	KY	P, H	fee title	315	permanent	6/14/2006
Acadiana Park Wetland Preservation	LA	P	fee title	25	permanent	6/21/2005
Chenier Plain Coastal Wetlands Conservation IV	LA, TX	P, H, O	fee title	1,162	permanent	3/8/2006
Chenier Plain Coastal Wetlands Conservation V	LA, TX	P, O	fee title	1,151	permanent	9/13/2006
Grand Cote NWR Wetland Enhancement	LA	P, H, O	easement	319	permanent	3/14/2007
Lower Mississippi Valley Ecosystem IV	LA, MS, AR	P, H, O	easement	1,400	permanent	9/13/2006
Lower Neches River Cypress	LA, TX	P, O	fee title	2,950	permanent	3/14/2007
Maurepas/Pontchartrain Habitat Conservation II	LA	P	fee title	7,600	permanent	9/21/2005
Maurepas/Pontchartrain Habitat Conservation III	LA	P	fee title	2,530	permanent	3/14/2007
Private Lands in the Lower Mississippi Valley & Gulf Coastal Plain II	LA, MS, AR	P, H	easement	6,698	permanent	9/21/2005
Sabine Island WMA - Acquisition Effort	LA	P	fee title	600	permanent	3/8/2006
Buzzards Bay Watershed: Dike Creek	MA	P, H, O	fee title	53	permanent	9/13/2006
			easement	199	permanent	
Buzzards Bay Watershed: Inner Bay Restoration & Edmunds	MA	P, H, O	fee title	102	permanent	9/13/2006
Buzzards Bay Watershed: Nasketucket Bay II	MA	P	fee title	106	permanent	9/21/2005
			easement	70	permanent	
Buzzards Bay Watershed: Slocums River	MA	P, O	easement	93	permanent	9/13/2006
Buzzards Bay Watershed: Westport River	MA	P	easement	207	permanent	9/21/2005
Buzzards Bay Wetlands Project	MA	P, O	fee title	10	permanent	6/13/2007
			easement	10	permanent	
Fitzgerald Lake Conservation Area & Saw Mill Hills Conservation Area	MA	P	fee title	100	permanent	6/21/2005
Pocomoke River Conservation Partnership 1	MD	P, H	easement	1,188	permanent	9/13/2006
Big Hill & Second Pond Forest Reserve	ME	P, O	easement	1,609	permanent	6/14/2006
Blaisdell - Clough I on the York River	ME	P	agreements	25	permanent	6/21/2005
Caribou Bog/Katahdin Iron Works	ME	P	easement	3,070	permanent	6/14/2006
Conserving a Network of Wetlands in the Tatnics: Tatnic Woods III	ME	P	fee title	29	permanent	6/21/2005
Greater Pleasant Bay Project Area II	ME	P	fee title	651	permanent	9/13/2006
			easement	25	permanent	
Greater York River Project Area	ME	P	fee title	484	permanent	9/21/2005
			easement	450	permanent	
Kennebec Estuary, Maine Phase II	ME	P, O	fee title	631	permanent	9/13/2006
Machias River Project	ME	P	fee title	7,785	permanent	9/21/2005
Northeast Penjajawoc Property Acquisition	ME	P	fee title	83	permanent	6/14/2006
Northern Corea Heath Acquisition	ME	P	fee title	606	permanent	6/14/2006
Richardson Seal Cove Property Acquisition	ME	P	fee title	43	permanent	6/21/2005
Sucker Brook Project	ME	P	fee title	227	permanent	6/14/2006
Upper Saco River Project: Hancock I	ME	P	easement	408	permanent	6/21/2005
Gateway to the Jordan River	MI	P	fee title	110	permanent	6/13/2007
Saginaw Bay to Lake Erie Coastal Habitat Project	MI	P, H, O	fee title	965	permanent	9/21/2005
Saint Clair Lake/Six Mile Lake Natural Area Addition	MI	P	fee title	51	permanent	6/13/2007
Wetland Property Acquisition for Migratory Birds	MI	P, O	fee title	82	permanent	6/21/2005

Multistate projects are listed in each state where they occur. Full figures are given with each listing.

U.S. North American Wetlands Conservation Act Projects Arrayed by State Conservation Mechanisms in Fiscal Years 2006-2007
[Section 10(1)(D)]

Project Title	State	Project Type	Conservation Mechanisms	Acres	Years Duration	Date Approved
Border Prairie Wetlands	MN	P, H, O	fee title	837	permanent	9/13/2006
			easement	493	permanent	
Geneva Lake Conservation Easements	MN	P, O	easement	250	permanent	6/14/2006
Lower Minnesota Prairie Coteau	MN	P, H, O	fee title	65	permanent	6/14/2006
Lower Minnesota Valley Wetland Conservation	MN	P, H, O	fee title	834	permanent	3/8/2006
Minnesota Headwaters I	MN	P, H, O	fee title	350	permanent	9/13/2006
			easement	458	permanent	
Rapids Lake Acquisition & Restoration Project	MN	P, H	fee title	116	permanent	6/21/2005
Roberts Waterfowl Production Area Restoration	MN	P, H	fee title	280	permanent	6/21/2005
Upper Minnesota River Valley Phase I	MN	P, H, O	fee title	1,504	permanent	3/14/2007
			easement	50	permanent	
Lewis & Clark Floodplain Heritage Partnership III	MO	P, H	fee title	176	permanent	9/13/2006
			easement	1,007	permanent	
Lower Mississippi Valley Ecosystem IV	MS, AR, LA	P, H, O	easement	1,400	permanent	9/13/2006
Malmaison WMA Forested Wetlands Enhancement	MS	P, H, O	easement	1,129	permanent	9/13/2006
Private Lands in the Lower Mississippi Valley & Gulf Coastal Plain II	MS, AR, LA	P, H	easement	6,698	permanent	9/21/2005
Lower Clark Fork River/Lake Pend Oreille Watershed	MT, ID	P, H, O	fee title	1,294	permanent	3/14/2007
			easement	1,243	permanent	
Madison/Gallatin Wetlands Conservation Project I	MT	P, H	easement	5,867	permanent	3/8/2006
Madison/Gallatin Wetlands Conservation Project II	MT	P, H	easement	2,958	permanent	3/14/2007
North Carolina Onslow Bight Partnership II	NC	P, H, O	fee title	6,425	permanent	9/21/2005
			easement	4,000	permanent	
Roanoke River Migratory Bird Initiative II	NC, VA	P, H, O	fee title	115	permanent	3/8/2006
			easement	340	permanent	
			lease	77	26 - 99	
Sound Investment Phase II	NC, VA	P, H, O	fee title	3,272	permanent	9/21/2005
			easement	186	permanent	
Suggs Millpond Game Land Managed Wetlands Enhancement Project	NC	P, H	fee title	53	permanent	6/21/2005
Chase Lake Area Wetland Project VII	ND	P, H, O	easement	6,265	permanent	9/13/2006
			lease	24,932	< 10 - 99	
Missouri Coteau Habitat Conservation Project IV	ND	P, O	easement	11,300	permanent	9/21/2005
			lease	7,145	10	
Missouri Coteau Habitat Conservation Project V	ND	P, O	easement	13,332	permanent	9/13/2006
			lease	8,083	< 10	
Mouse River Watershed Enhancement Project V	ND	P, H, O	easement	9,751	26 - permanent	3/8/2006
			lease	7,542	< 10	
North Dakota Drift Prairie Project I	ND	P, H, O	fee title	158	permanent	9/13/2006
			easement	3,344	permanent	
			lease	17,083	< 10 - 99	
North Dakota Great Plains Project V	ND	P, H, O	easement	3,333	permanent	3/14/2007
			lease	14,624	< 10	
Northern Coteau Project V	ND	P, H, O	easement	5,586	permanent	9/21/2005
			lease	15,053	10	

Multistate projects are listed in each state where they occur. Full figures are given with each listing.

U.S. North American Wetlands Conservation Act Projects Arrayed by State
Conservation Mechanisms in Fiscal Years 2006-2007
[Section 10(1)(D)]

Project Title	State	Project Type	Conservation Mechanisms	Acres	Years Duration	Date Approved
Big Bend Reach of the Platte River Phase I	NE	P, H, O	fee title	790	permanent	3/14/2007
			easement	500	permanent	
Middle Missouri River II	NE, IA	P, H, O	fee title	4,090	permanent	3/8/2006
Rainwater Basin Habitat Conservation Project II	NE	P, H, O	easement	478	permanent	3/14/2007
			lease	347	< 10 - 25	
Great Bay Estuary VI: Piscassic River Watershed	NH	P, O	fee title	118	permanent	3/14/2007
			easement	546	permanent	
Piscassic Greenway Conservation Initiative	NH	P	easement	329	permanent	6/21/2005
Robb Reservoir Landscape Conservation Project	NH	P	fee title	3	permanent	6/14/2006
			easement	1,668	permanent	
Wapack Wilderness Conservation Campaign	NH	P	fee title	1,400	permanent	6/13/2007
Acquisition & Protection of Private Property within Wetland Complex	NY	P, H, O	fee title	15	permanent	6/21/2005
Saint Lawrence River Valley I	NY	P, H, O	fee title	1,607	permanent	9/21/2005
			easement	2,613	permanent	
Ohio Grand River Wetlands Project	OH	P, H, O	fee title	347	permanent	9/21/2005
			easement	1,294	permanent	
Shaffer Playa, Oklahoma	OK	P, O	fee title	212	permanent	6/14/2006
Lower Columbia River Ecoregion IV	OR, WA	P, H, O	fee title	989	permanent	3/8/2006
		lease		109	26 - 99	
Lower Columbia River Estuary Project II	OR, WA	P, H	fee title	30	permanent	9/21/2005
			easement	375	permanent	
			lease	31	26 - 99	
Lower Yaquina Salt Marsh Conservation Project	OR	P, O	fee title	41	permanent	6/14/2006
			easement	35	permanent	
Upper Klamath Lakes Wetlands	OR	P, H, O	fee title	2,820	permanent	9/13/2006
			easement	2,525	permanent	
Upper Willamette Wetlands Conservation Initiative II	OR	P, H	easement	1,271	permanent	3/14/2007
Willamette River Delta Restoration Phase I	OR	P, H, O	fee title	369	permanent	3/14/2007
Buzzards Bay Watershed: Tiverton Great Swamp	RI	P, O	easement	230	permanent	9/13/2006
Ace Basin: Edisto River Corridor Protection Project II	SC	P, O	fee title	2,560	permanent	9/21/2005
			easement	1,841	permanent	
South Carolina Pee Dee River Conservation Initiative: Woodbury Tract	SC	P	fee title	25,668	permanent	9/13/2006
South Carolina Savannah River Conservation Initiative: Hamilton Ridge Tract	SC	P	fee title	13,281	permanent	9/13/2006
James River Lowlands/Missouri Coteau Project II	SD	P, O	fee title	1,830	permanent	3/8/2006
			easement	6,596	permanent	
James River Lowlands/Missouri Coteau Project III	SD	P, O	easement	6,081	permanent	3/14/2007

Multistate projects are listed in each state where they occur. Full figures are given with each listing.

U.S. North American Wetlands Conservation Act Projects Arrayed by State Conservation Mechanisms in Fiscal Years 2006-2007 [Section 10(1)(D)]

Project Title	State	Project Type	Conservation Mechanisms	Acres	Years Duration	Date Approved
Big Swan Headwaters Preserve: Boiling Springs Tract	TN	P, H	fee title	27	permanent	6/13/2007
Lower Obion River III	TN	P, H, O	fee title	1,325	permanent	3/8/2006
Restoration of Lick Creek Wetlands - Joachim Bible Refuge Tracts	TN	P, H	fee title	273	permanent	6/14/2006
Wolf River, Tennessee Phase II	TN	P, H	fee title	2,351	permanent	3/14/2007
			easement	60	permanent	
Austins Woods III	TX	P	fee title	564	permanent	3/14/2007
			easement	313	permanent	
Chenier Plain Coastal Wetlands Conservation IV	TX, LA	P, H, O	fee title	1,162	permanent	3/8/2006
Chenier Plain Coastal Wetlands Conservation V	TX, LA	P, O	fee title	1,151	permanent	9/13/2006
Coastal Prairie Wetlands Restoration & Acquisition	TX	P, H	fee title	6,618	permanent	9/21/2005
			easement	360	permanent	
Gulf Coast JV Mottled Duck Conservation Plan	TX	P, H	easement	160	permanent	6/13/2007
Lower Neches River Cypress	TX, LA	P, O	fee title	2,950	permanent	3/14/2007
Lower Rappahannock Phase III	VA	P	fee title	1,280	permanent	3/8/2006
			easement	2,217	permanent	
Roanoke River Migratory Bird Initiative II	VA, NC	P, H, O	fee title	115	permanent	3/8/2006
			easement	340	permanent	
			lease	77	26 - 99	
Sound Investment Phase II	VA, NC	P, H, O	fee title	3,272	permanent	9/21/2005
			easement	186	permanent	
Southern Tip Cooperative Conservation Initiative	VA	P, H	fee title	578	permanent	9/13/2006
			easement	1,294	permanent	
Chehalis River Floodplain & Estuary Wetland Conservation	WA	P, H, O	fee title	1,380	permanent	3/8/2006
			easement	1,582	permanent	
Crow Marsh Project/Crow Marsh East	WA	P, H, O	fee title	7	permanent	6/13/2007
			easement	7	permanent	
Lower Columbia River Ecoregion IV	WA, OR	P, H, O	fee title	989	permanent	3/8/2006
		lease	109	26 - 99		
Lower Columbia River Estuary Project II	WA, OR	P, H	fee title	30	permanent	9/21/2005
			easement	375	permanent	
		lease	31	26 - 99		
Lower Yakima Wetlands Protection/Restoration II	WA	P, H, O	fee title	320	permanent	9/13/2006
Lummi Island Conservation Project	WA	P	easement	436	permanent	6/14/2006
Middle Puget Sound Wetlands Phase I	WA	P, H, O	fee title	69	permanent	9/21/2005
			easement	118	permanent	
North Willapa Bay Wetlands Conservation	WA	P, H, O	fee title	1,391	permanent	9/13/2006
Otto Preserve Expansion Project	WA	P, O	fee title	24	permanent	6/21/2005
Hawk Metals Wetland Acquisition	WI	P	fee title	720	permanent	6/14/2006
Leopold Memorial Reserve - Migratory Habitat Expansion	WI	P, H, O	fee title	15	permanent	6/21/2005
Lower Chippewa River Wetland Protection Partnership II	WI	P, H, O	fee title	2,166	permanent	3/8/2006
		easement	470	permanent		
Southcentral Wisconsin Prairie Pothole Initiative III	WI	P, H, O	fee title	2,478	permanent	9/21/2005
		easement	430	permanent		
The Des Plaines River Lowlands Conservation Project	WI	P, H, O	fee title	38	permanent	6/13/2007
Whitefish Lake & Wetland Preservation	WI	P	easement	37	permanent	6/21/2005

Multistate projects are listed in each state where they occur. Full figures are given with each listing.

Canadian North American Wetlands Conservation Act Projects Arrayed by Province
Conservation Mechanisms in Fiscal Years 2006-2007
[Section 10(1)(D)]

Project Title	Province/ Territory	Project Type	Conservation Mechanisms	Acres	Years Duration	Date Approved
Alberta Habitat Program	AB, BC	P, H, O	fee title	218	permanent	9/21/2005
			agreements*	956	10 - permanent	
Canadian Intermountain JV & Pacific Coast JV Wetland - Associated Migratory Bird Habitat	AB, BC	P, H, O	fee title	345	permanent	9/21/2005
Canadian Intermountain JV & Pacific Coast JV Wetland - Associated Migratory Bird Habitat	AB, BC	P, H, O	fee title	181	permanent	6/14/2006
Canadian Intermountain JV & Pacific Coast JV Wetland - Associated Migratory Bird Habitat	AB, BC	P, H, O	fee title	179	permanent	6/13/2007
Critical Wetland & Upland Habitat - Alberta	AB	P, H, O	fee title	500	permanent	9/21/2005
			easement	4,000	permanent	
Potholes Plus Project	AB, MB	P, H, O	easement	5,600	permanent	9/21/2005
Potholes Plus Project	AB, MB, SK	P, H, O	easement	6,680	permanent	6/13/2007
Prairie - Western Boreal Region Habitat Program	AB, BC, MB, NT, SK, YT	P, H, O	fee title	4,844	permanent	6/14/2006
			agreements*	57,112	30 - permanent	
Prairie - Western Boreal Region Habitat Program	AB, BC, MB, NT, SK, YT	P, H, O	fee title	1,586	permanent	9/13/2006
			agreements*	18,694	10 - permanent	
Prairie - Western Boreal Region Habitat Program	AB, BC, MB,T NT, SK, YT	P, H, O	fee title	3,687	permanent	6/13/2007
			agreements*	53,719	10 - permanent	
Prairie Canada Wetlands & Uplands	AB, SK	P, H, O	fee title	1,300	permanent	6/14/2006
			easement	13,500	permanent	
Prairie Canada Wetlands & Uplands	AB, MB, SK	P, H, O	fee title	2,160	permanent	6/13/2007
			agreements*	11,740	permanent	
Alberta Habitat Program	BC, AB	P, H, O	fee title	218	permanent	9/21/2005
			agreements*	956	10 - permanent	
Canadian Intermountain JV & Pacific Coast JV Wetland - Associated Migratory Bird Habitat	BC, AB	P, H, O	fee title	345	permanent	9/21/2005
Canadian Intermountain JV & Pacific Coast JV Wetland - Associated Migratory Bird Habitat	BC, AB	P, H, O	fee title	181	permanent	6/14/2006
Canadian Intermountain JV & Pacific Coast JV Wetland - Associated Migratory Bird Habitat	BC, AB	P, H, O	fee title	179	permanent	6/13/2007
Critical Wetlands & Associated Upland Habitats	BC	P, H, O	fee title	43	permanent	9/21/2005
			agreements*	810	10 - permanent	
Critical Wetlands & Associated Upland Habitats	BC	P, H, O	fee title	475	permanent	6/14/2006
			agreements*	945	10 - permanent	
Critical Wetlands & Associated Upland Habitats	BC	P, H, O	fee title	260	permanent	9/13/2006
			agreements*	230	30 - permanent	
Critical Wetlands & Associated Upland Habitats	BC	P, H, O	fee title	535	permanent	6/13/2007
			agreements*	400	30 - permanent	
Prairie - Western Boreal Region Habitat Program	BC, AB, MB, NT, SK, YT	P, H, O	fee title	4,844	permanent	6/14/2006
			agreements*	57,112	30 - permanent	
Prairie - Western Boreal Region Habitat Program	BC, AB, MB NT, SK, YT	P, H, O	fee title	1,586	permanent	9/13/2006
			agreements*	18,694	10 - permanent	
Prairie - Western Boreal Region Habitat Program	BC, AB, MB, NT, SK, YT	P, H, O	fee title	3,687	permanent	6/13/2007
			agreements*	53,719	10 - permanent	

Multistate projects are listed in each province/territory where they occur. Full figures are given with each listing.
Agreements are undifferentiated combinations of leases, easements, and management agreements.

Canadian North American Wetlands Conservation Act Projects Arrayed by Province
Conservation Mechanisms in Fiscal Years 2006-2007
[Section 10(1)(D)]

Project Title	Province/ Territory	Project Type	Conservation Mechanisms	Acres	Years Duration	Date Approved
Manitoba Critical Wetland & Upland Habitat	MB	P, H, O	fee title	320	permanent	9/21/2005
			agreements	1,920	permanent	
Potholes Plus Project	MB, AB	P, H, O	easement	5,600	permanent	9/21/2005
Potholes Plus Project	MB, AB, SK	P, H, O	easement	6,680	permanent	6/13/2007
Prairie - Western Boreal Region Habitat Program	MB, AB, BC, NT, SK, YT	P, H, O	fee title	4,844	permanent	6/14/2006
			agreements*	57,112	30 - permanent	
Prairie - Western Boreal Region Habitat Program	MB, AB, BC, NT, SK, YT	P, H, O	fee title	1,586	permanent	9/13/2006
			agreements*	18,694	10 - permanent	
Prairie - Western Boreal Region Habitat Program	MB, AB, BC, NT, SK, YT	P, H, O	fee title	3,687	permanent	6/13/2007
			agreements*	53,719	10 - permanent	
Prairie Canada Wetlands & Uplands	MB, AB, SK	P, H, O	fee title	2,160	permanent	6/13/2007
			agreements*	11,740	permanent	
Atlantic Canada Wetland Securement Project	NB, NF	P, H, O	fee title	200	permanent	9/21/2005
Atlantic Canada Wetlands Conservation	NB, NF, NS	P, H, O	fee title	204	permanent	9/21/2005
			agreements	1,275	30	
Atlantic Coastal Waterfowl Habitat Conservation	NB, PE	P, H, O	fee title	500	permanent	6/13/2007
			easement	1,000	permanent	
Eastern Habitat JV Wetlands Conservation	NB, NF, NS, ON, PE, QC	P, H, O	fee title	3,074	permanent	6/14/2006
			agreements	3,899	30	
Eastern Habitat JV Wetlands Conservation	NB, NF, NS, ON, PE, QC	P, H, O	fee title	2,121	permanent	9/13/2006
			agreements	936	30	
Eastern Habitat JV Wetlands Conservation	NB, NF, NS, ON, PE, QC	P, H, O	fee title	1,500	permanent	6/13/2007
			agreements	1,910	30	
Maritimes Wetland Securement Project	NB, NS, PE	P, H, O	fee title	500	permanent	6/14/2006
Atlantic Canada Wetland Securement Project	NF, NB	P, H, O	fee title	200	permanent	9/21/2005
Atlantic Canada Wetlands Conservation	NF, NB, NS	P, H, O	fee title	204	permanent	9/21/2005
			agreements	1,275	30	
Eastern Habitat JV Wetlands Conservation	NF, NB, NS, ON, PE, QC	P, H, O	fee title	3,074	permanent	6/14/2006
			agreements	3,899	30	
Eastern Habitat JV Wetlands Conservation	NF, NB, NS, ON, PE, QC	P, H, O	fee title	2,121	permanent	9/13/2006
			agreements	936	30	
Eastern Habitat JV Wetlands Conservation	NF, NB, NS, ON, PE, QC	P, H, O	fee title	1,500	permanent	6/13/2007
			agreements	1,910	30	
Atlantic Canada Wetlands Conservation	NS, NB, NF	P, H, O	fee title	204	permanent	9/21/2005
			agreements	1,275	30	
Eastern Habitat JV Wetlands Conservation	NS, NB, NF, ON, PE, QC	P, H, O	fee title	3,074	permanent	6/14/2006
			agreements	3,899	30	
Eastern Habitat JV Wetlands Conservation	NS, NB, NF, ON, PE, QC	P, H, O	fee title	2,121	permanent	9/13/2006
			agreements	936	30	
Eastern Habitat JV Wetlands Conservation	NS, NB, NF, ON, PE, QC	P, H, O	fee title	1,500	permanent	6/13/2007
			agreements	1,910	30	
Maritimes Wetland Securement Project	NS, NB, PE	P, H, O	fee title	500	permanent	6/14/2006

Multistate projects are listed in each provice/territory where they occur. Full figures are given with each listing.
Agreements are undifferentiated combinations of leases, easements, and management agreements.

23

Canadian North American Wetlands Conservation Act Projects Arrayed by Province
Conservation Mechanisms in Fiscal Years 2006-2007
[Section 10(1)(D)]

Project Title	Province/ Territory	Project Type	Conservation Mechanisms	Acres	Years Duration	Date Approved
Prairie - Western Boreal Region Habitat Program	NT, AB, BC, MB, SK, YT	P, H, O	fee title agreements*	4,844 57,112	permanent 30 - permanent	6/14/2006
Prairie - Western Boreal Region Habitat Program	NT, AB, BC, MB, SK, YT	P, H, O	fee title agreements*	1,586 18,694	permanent 10 - permanent	9/13/2006
Prairie - Western Boreal Region Habitat Program	NT, AB, BC, MB, SK, YT	P, H, O	fee title agreements*	3,687 53,719	permanent 10 - permanent	6/13/2007
Ducks Unlimited Canada Ontario Project	ON	P, H, O	fee title agreements*	25 257	permanent 20 - permanent	9/21/2005
Eastern Habitat JV Wetlands Conservation	ON, NB, NF, NS, PE, QC	P, H, O	fee title agreements	3,074 3,899	permanent 30	6/14/2006
Eastern Habitat JV Wetlands Conservation	ON, NB, NF, NS, PE, QC	P, H, O	fee title agreements	2,121 936	permanent 30	9/13/2006
Eastern Habitat JV Wetlands Conservation	ON, NB, NF, NS, PE, QC	P, H, O	fee title agreements	1,500 1,910	permanent 30	6/13/2007
Great Lakes Wetlands Habitat Conservation Project	ON	P, H, O	fee title easement	60 40	permanent permanent	9/21/2005
Ontario Wetland Habitat Fund Program	ON	P, H, O	agreements	4,319	10+	9/21/2005
Atlantic Coastal Waterfowl Habitat Conservation	PE, NB	P, H, O	fee title easement	500 1,000	permanent permanent	6/13/2007
Eastern Habitat JV Wetlands Conservation	PE, NB, NF, NS, ON, QC	P, H, O	fee title agreements	3,074 3,899	permanent 30	6/14/2006
Eastern Habitat JV Wetlands Conservation	PE, NB, NF, NS, ON, QC	P, H, O	fee title agreements	2,121 936	permanent 30	9/13/2006
Eastern Habitat JV Wetlands Conservation	PE, NB, NF, NS, ON, QC	P, H, O	fee title agreements	1,500 1,910	permanent 30	6/13/2007
Maritimes Wetland Securement Project	PE, NB, NS	P, H, O	fee title	500	permanent	6/14/2006
Eastern Habitat JV Wetlands Conservation	QC, NB, NF, NS, ON, PE	P, H, O	fee title agreements	3,074 3,899	permanent 30	6/14/2006
Eastern Habitat JV Wetlands Conservation	QC, NB, NF, NS, ON, PE	P, H, O	fee title agreements	2,121 936	permanent 30	9/13/2006
Eastern Habitat JV Wetlands Conservation	QC, NB, NF, NS, ON, PE	P, H, O	fee title agreements	1,500 1,910	permanent 30	6/13/2007
Quebec: Protecting Wetland & Upland Habitat	QC	P, H, O	fee title easement	699 612	permanent permanent	6/14/2006
Quebec: Protecting Wetland & Upland Habitat	QC	P, H, O	fee title easement	298 16	permanent permanent	9/13/2006
Quebec: Protecting Wetland & Upland Habitat	QC	P, H, O	fee title easement	810 50	permanent permanent	6/13/2007
Quebec/Saint Lawrence Watershed	QC	P, H, O	fee title agreements	550 200	permanent 25	9/21/2005
Saint Lawrence River & Lake Champlain Critical Wetland Habitat Project	QC	P, H, O	fee title	200	permanent	9/21/2005

Multistate projects are listed in each province/territory where they occur. Full figures are given with each listing.
Agreements are undifferentiated combinations of leases, easements, and management agreements.

Canadian North American Wetlands Conservation Act Projects Arrayed by Province
Conservation Mechanisms in Fiscal Years 2006-2007
[Section 10(1)(D)]

Project Title	Province/ Territory	Project Type	Conservation Mechanisms	Acres	Years Duration	Date Approved
Potholes Plus Project	SK, AB, MB	P, H, O	easement	6,680	permanent	6/13/2007
Prairie - Western Boreal Region Habitat Program	SK, AB, BC, MB, NT, YT	P, H, O	fee title agreements*	4,844 57,112	permanent 30 - permanent	6/14/2006
Prairie - Western Boreal Region Habitat Program	SK, AB, BC, MB, NT, YT	P, H, O	fee title agreements*	1,586 18,694	permanent 10 - permanent	9/13/2006
Prairie - Western Boreal Region Habitat Program	SK, AB, BC, MB, NT, YT	P, H, O	fee title agreements*	3,687 53,719	permanent 10 - permanent	6/13/2007
Prairie Canada Wetlands & Uplands	SK, AB	P, H, O	fee title easement	1,300 13,500	permanent permanent	6/14/2006
Prairie Canada Wetlands & Uplands	SK, AB, MB	P, H, O	fee title agreements*	2,160 11,740	permanent permanent	6/13/2007
Saskatchewan Habitat Program	SK	P, H, O	fee title agreements*	45 2,147	permanent 10 - permanent	9/21/2005
Saskatchewan Wetlands & Uplands	SK	P, H, O	fee title easement	350 3,650	permanent permanent	9/21/2005
Prairie - Western Boreal Region Habitat Program	YT, AB, BC, MB, NT, SK	P, H, O	fee title agreements*	4,844 57,112	permanent 30 - permanent	6/14/2006
Prairie - Western Boreal Region Habitat Program	YT, AB, BC, MB, NT, SK	P, H, O	fee title agreements*	1,586 18,694	permanent 10 - permanent	9/13/2006
Prairie - Western Boreal Region Habitat Program	YT, AB, BC, MB, NT, SK	P, H, O	fee title agreements*	3,687 53,719	permanent 10 - permanent	6/13/2007

Multistate projects are listed in each provice/territory where they occur. Full figures are given with each listing.
Agreements are undifferentiated combinations of leases, easements, and management agreements.

Mexican North American Wetlands Conservation Act Projects Arrayed by State Conservation Mechanisms in Fiscal Years 2006-2007
[Section 10(1)(D)]

Project Title	State	Project Type	Conservation Mechanisms	Acres	Years Duration	Date Approved
Implementation of Legal Conservation Mechanisms in Laguna San Ignacio II	BCS	P	easement	6,669	permanent	3/14/2007
Waterfowl Reserve Network In Northwest Chihuahua	CHIH	P, H, O	easement	7,413	20 - renewable	3/8/2006
Protection, Management & Rehabilation of Lajoya - Buenavista & Manguito - Chocohuital Wetlands	CHIS	P, H	agreements	2,965	10 - renewable	3/14/2007
Waterfowl Refuges in Cuatrocienegas, Coahuila	COAH	P, H	easement	11,119	20 - renewable	3/8/2006
Conservation of Wintering Areas for Migratory Waterfowl & Shorebirds in Sonora & Sinaloa	SIN, SON	P, H, O	agreements	124	< 10 - permanent	3/14/2007
Conservation of Wintering Areas for Migratory Waterfowl & Shorebirds in Sonora & Sinaloa	SON, SIN	P, H, O	agreements	124	< 10 - permanent	3/14/2007
Protection of Sea Grasses for the Conservation of Waterfowl in Laguna Madre	TAMPS	P, O	agreements	86,765	30	3/14/2007
Restoration of Wetlands & Land Purchase in the Rio Grande Delta	TAMPS	P, H	fee title agreements	4,943 903	permanent permanent	3/14/2007

Multistate projects are listed in each state where they occur. Full figures are given with each listing.

Financial Statements
[Section 10(2)]

Fiscal Year 2006

Receipts

FY 2006 Interest	$12,410,937
FY 2005 Interest Carryover	$1,248,018
FY 2006 Appropriation	$39,411,504
FY 2005 Appropriation Carryover	$2,168,032
FY 2006 Fines, Penalties, Forfeitures	$799,629
FY 2005 Fines, Penalties, Forfeitures Carryover	$4,435,000
FY 2006 Coastal Funds	$13,512,781
FY 2005 Coastal Funds Carryover	$261,246
Total	**$74,247,147**

Debits

Administration	$2,645,394
Project Obligations:	
United States	$42,400,192
Canada	$22,732,734
Mexico	$2,530,405
Total	**$70,308,725**

Fiscal Year 2007

Receipts

FY 2007 Interest	$14,175,522
FY 2006 Interest Carryover	$75,957
FY 2007 Appropriation	$39,411,504
FY 2006 Appropriation Carryover	$1,465,806
FY 2007 Fines, Penalties, Forfeitures	$480,886
FY 2006 Fines, Penalties, Forfeitures Carryover	$2,435,000
FY 2007 Coastal Funds	$16,372,044
FY 2006 Coastal Funds Carryover	$3,514,907
Total	**$77,931,626**

Debits

Administration	$2,817,600
Project Obligations:	
United States	$46,871,251
Canada	$23,357,337
Mexico	$2,610,736
Total	**$75,656,924**

U.S. North American Wetlands Conservation Act Projects Arrayed by State
Federal and Partner Dollars Invested in Fiscal Years 2006-2007
[Section 10(2)]

Project Title	State/ Territory	Project Type	Grant Amount	Partner Amount	Total Amount	Date Approved
Chena Flats Greenbelt Project	AK	P	$50,000	$159,360	$209,360	6/21/2005
Chena Flats Greenbelt Project - Ketzler Property	AK	P	$75,000	$115,450	$190,450	6/14/2006
Potter Marsh State Wildlife Refuge Protection Project	AK	P	$50,000	$224,000	$274,000	6/21/2005
Total			$175,000	$498,810	$673,810	
Bottomland Conservation in the Arkansas Delta	AR	P, H	$917,140	$1,834,281	$2,751,421	3/8/2006
Lower Mississippi Valley Ecosystem IV	AR, LA, MS	P, H, O	$1,000,000	$2,442,615	$3,442,615	9/13/2006
Private Lands in the Lower Mississippi Valley & Gulf Coastal Plain II	AR, LA, MS	P, H	$495,000	$5,729,797	$6,224,797	9/21/2005
Total			$2,412,140	$10,006,693	$12,418,833	
Cibola NWR Wetlands Project	AZ	H, O	$46,000	$376,200	$422,200	6/13/2007
Sonoran Wetlands Restoration I	AZ, CA	P, H, O	$1,000,000	$2,642,610	$3,642,610	3/14/2007
Total			$1,046,000	$3,018,810	$4,064,810	
Burton Property - Litchfield Habitat Restoration & Enhancement Project	CA	H	$36,700	$143,297	$179,997	6/21/2005
Butte & Colusa Basins Wetlands Project	CA	P, H, O	$1,000,000	$5,054,979	$6,054,979	3/14/2007
Coastal Marin Wetlands Restoration Project I	CA	H, O	$999,007	$2,301,367	$3,300,374	9/13/2006
Elmwood Tract Phase I	CA	H	$74,882	$92,882	$167,764	6/13/2007
Freshwater Creek Estuary Rehabilitation Project	CA	H	$50,000	$572,030	$622,030	6/21/2005
Humboldt Bay Coastal Education Center & Reserve	CA	P, O	$75,000	$844,775	$919,775	6/13/2007
Janes Creek Log Pond Acquisition Project	CA	P, H	$50,000	$75,000	$125,000	6/21/2005
Mad River Slough Coastal Wetland Enhancement & Salt Marsh Restoration	CA	H	$75,000	$192,100	$267,100	6/13/2007
Modoc Plateau/Pit River Wetlands Project	CA	P, H, O	$1,000,000	$2,724,044	$3,724,044	3/8/2006
North Sacramento Valley Wetland Habitat Project II	CA	P, H, O	$1,000,000	$2,635,479	$3,635,479	9/21/2005
North San Joaquin Valley Wetland Habitat Project II	CA	P, H, O	$1,000,000	$2,967,986	$3,967,986	3/8/2006
Northern Tulare / San Joaquin Basins I	CA	P, H, O	$1,000,000	$2,323,714	$3,323,714	9/21/2005
San Dieguito Lepidium Latifolium Control Project	CA	H, O	$74,710	$162,579	$237,289	6/13/2007
San Joaquin Basin Wetland Restoration II	CA	H, O	$50,000	$90,005	$140,005	6/21/2005
Sonoran Wetlands Restoration I	CA, AZ	P, H, O	$1,000,000	$2,642,610	$3,642,610	3/14/2007
South San Francisco Bay Wetlands Restoration Project	CA	H, O	$1,000,000	$5,040,090	$6,040,090	9/13/2006
Yolo Basin Wetland Habitat Project III	CA	P, H, O	$1,000,000	$2,419,930	$3,419,930	3/14/2007
Total			$9,485,299	$30,282,867	$39,768,166	
Conservation of a Playa Complex in Eastern Colorado	CO	P, H, O	$11,550	$22,550	$34,100	6/21/2005
Huerfano Lake Conservation & Restoration Project	CO	H, O	$16,253	$34,453	$50,706	6/14/2006
Lower South Platte River Wetland & Riparian Restoration II	CO	P, H, O	$999,977	$4,773,637	$5,773,614	9/21/2005
Lower South Platte Wetland Initiative	CO	H, O	$75,000	$80,500	$155,500	6/14/2006
San Luis Valley Wetland Project III	CO	P, H, O	$1,000,000	$3,662,422	$4,662,422	3/8/2006
The Miller Ranch Preservation Project	CO	P, H	$75,000	$268,000	$343,000	6/14/2006
Total			$2,177,780	$8,841,562	$11,019,342	
Aton Forest Preservation Project	CT	P	$75,000	$234,900	$309,900	6/14/2006
Total			$75,000	$234,900	$309,900	

Multistate projects are listed in each state/territory where they occur. Full figures are given with each listing.

U.S. North American Wetlands Conservation Act Projects Arrayed by State
Federal and Partner Dollars Invested in Fiscal Years 2006-2007
[Section 10(2)]

Project Title	State/ Territory	Project Type	Grant Amount	Partner Amount	Total Amount	Date Approved
Invasive Species Eradication & Mangrove Planting in the Indian River Lagoon	FL	H, O	$22,053	$45,261	$67,314	6/21/2005
Total			**$22,053**	**$45,261**	**$67,314**	
Kauai Wetland Restoration Phase I	HI	P, H	$75,000	$279,327	$354,327	6/14/2006
Total			**$75,000**	**$279,327**	**$354,327**	
Cedar - Wapsi Valley Wetlands	IA	P	$1,000,000	$2,712,357	$3,712,357	9/13/2006
Central Iowa Protected Water Areas Wetland Conservation Project	IA	P	$75,000	$90,000	$165,000	6/14/2006
Iowa Living Lakes - Diamond Lake	IA	H, O	$50,000	$142,500	$192,500	6/21/2005
Iowa Prairie Pothole Upland Habitat Development II	IA	H	$75,000	$165,369	$240,369	6/14/2006
Middle Missouri River II	IA, NE	P, H, O	$1,000,000	$2,530,933	$3,530,933	3/8/2006
Mitchell County Wetland Habitat Development	IA	P, H	$50,000	$185,400	$235,400	6/21/2005
Prairie Lakes Wetland Initiative	IA	P, H, O	$1,000,000	$6,332,449	$7,332,449	3/14/2007
Total			**$3,250,000**	**$12,159,008**	**$15,409,008**	
Bear Lake Valley Wetlands Restoration	ID	H, O	$625,000	$1,692,552	$2,317,552	9/21/2005
Camas Creek Ranch	ID	H	$50,000	$636,665	$686,665	6/21/2005
Henry's Fork Wetlands II	ID	P, H	$1,000,000	$6,400,105	$7,400,105	9/21/2005
Lower Clark Fork River/Lake Pend Oreille Watershed	ID, MT	P, H, O	$1,000,000	$7,518,200	$8,518,200	3/14/2007
Total			**$2,675,000**	**$16,247,522**	**$18,922,522**	
Black Gold Nesting Habitat Enhancement Project	IL	H, O	$50,000	$50,000	$100,000	6/21/2005
Burning Star 5 Wetland Enhancement Project	IL	H, O	$23,750	$24,000	$47,750	6/14/2006
Michael Wolff Memorial Wetland Project	IL	H, O	$47,142	$50,725	$97,867	6/21/2005
Restoring a Large Native Prairie/Wetland Complex	IL	H, O	$50,000	$66,100	$116,100	6/21/2005
Total			**$170,892**	**$190,825**	**$361,717**	
Goose Pond Fish & Wildlife Area Moist Soil Enhancement Project	IN	P, H, O	$67,521	$103,677	$171,198	6/13/2007
Limberlost & Loblolly Wetland Restoration Project	IN	P, H, O	$35,750	$120,451	$156,201	6/21/2005
Total			**$103,271**	**$224,128**	**$327,399**	
Frazier Park Lake Restoration Project: Sediment Removal	KS	H	$50,000	$267,000	$317,000	6/21/2005
Jamestown Wildlife Area Phase I	KS	P, H, O	$999,345	$2,212,617	$3,211,962	3/8/2006
Total			**$1,049,345**	**$2,479,617**	**$3,528,962**	
Three Ponds State Nature Preserve Addition #1: Bottomland Hardwood	KY	P, H	$50,000	$447,500	$497,500	6/14/2006
Total			**$50,000**	**$447,500**	**$497,500**	

Multistate projects are listed in each state/territory where they occur. Full figures are given with each listing.

U.S. North American Wetlands Conservation Act Projects Arrayed by State
Federal and Partner Dollars Invested in Fiscal Years 2006-2007
[Section 10(2)]

Project Title	State/ Territory	Project Type	Grant Amount	Partner Amount	Total Amount	Date Approved
Acadiana Park Wetland Preservation	LA	P	$50,000	$56,000	$106,000	6/21/2005
Chenier Plain - Additional Funds For Hurricane Damage	LA	O	$206,000	$0	$206,000	3/8/2006
Chenier Plain Coastal Wetlands Conservation IV	LA, TX	P, H, O	$637,771	$1,593,624	$2,231,395	3/8/2006
Chenier Plain Coastal Wetlands Conservation V	LA, TX	P, O	$1,000,000	$3,005,040	$4,005,040	9/13/2006
Grand Cote NWR Wetland Enhancement	LA	P, H, O	$685,114	$1,753,077	$2,438,191	3/14/2007
Gulf Coast Wetlands Restoration & Enhancement	LA	P, H, O	$999,460	$2,475,633	$3,475,093	3/14/2007
Lafitte Terracing Project	LA	H, O	$439,182	$893,315	$1,332,497	3/8/2006
Louisiana Coastal Wetlands III	LA	P, H	$995,500	$2,329,455	$3,324,955	9/21/2005
Lower Mississippi Valley Ecosystem IV	LA, AR, MS	P, H, O	$1,000,000	$2,442,615	$3,442,615	9/13/2006
Lower Neches River Cypress	LA, TX	P, O	$932,200	$3,104,640	$4,036,840	3/14/2007
Maurepas/Pontchartrain Habitat Conservation II	LA	P	$1,000,000	$3,774,000	$4,774,000	9/21/2005
Maurepas/Pontchartrain Habitat Conservation III	LA	P	$950,000	$2,095,000	$3,045,000	3/14/2007
Pointe - Aux - Chenes - Additional Funds For Hurricane Damage	LA	O	$161,750	$0	$161,750	3/8/2006
Private Lands in the Lower Mississippi Valley & Gulf Coastal Plain II	LA, AR, MS	P, H	$495,000	$5,729,797	$6,224,797	9/21/2005
Sabine Island WMA - Acquisition Effort	LA	P	$800,000	$2,470,000	$3,270,000	3/8/2006
Total			**$10,351,977**	**$31,722,196**	**$42,074,173**	
Buzzards Bay Watershed: Dike Creek	MA	P, H, O	$1,000,000	$1,887,000	$2,887,000	9/13/2006
Buzzards Bay Watershed: Inner Bay Restoration & Edmunds	MA	P, H, O	$800,000	$1,840,711	$2,640,711	9/13/2006
Buzzards Bay Watershed: Nasketucket Bay II	MA	P	$1,000,000	$2,210,000	$3,210,000	9/21/2005
Buzzards Bay Watershed: Slocums River	MA	P, O	$300,000	$1,200,000	$1,500,000	9/13/2006
Buzzards Bay Watershed: Westport River	MA	P	$1,000,000	$2,335,000	$3,335,000	9/21/2005
Buzzards Bay Wetlands Project	MA	P, O	$35,000	$35,000	$70,000	6/13/2007
Fitzgerald Lake Conservation Area & Saw Mill Hills Conservation Area	MA	P	$50,000	$62,000	$112,000	6/21/2005
Upper Great Marsh Tidal Marsh Restoration	MA	H, O	$45,000	$45,200	$90,200	6/14/2006
Wetland Habitat Restoration at Woodbridge Island	MA	H, O	$58,740	$63,500	$122,240	6/13/2007
Total			**$4,288,740**	**$9,678,411**	**$13,967,151**	
Allegheny Mountain - Northern Ridge & Valley	MD, VA, WV	H, O	$75,000	$215,589	$290,589	6/13/2007
E.A. Vaughn WMA Wetland Restoration Project	MD	H, O	$39,000	$55,630	$94,630	6/21/2005
Pocomoke River Conservation Partnership I	MD	P, H	$648,727	$1,450,169	$2,098,896	9/13/2006
Total			**$762,727**	**$1,721,388**	**$2,484,115**	

Multistate projects are listed in each state/territory where they occur. Full figures are given with each listing.

U.S. North American Wetlands Conservation Act Projects Arrayed by State
Federal and Partner Dollars Fiscal Years Invested in 2006-2007
[Section 10(2)]

Project Title	State/ Territory	Project Type	Grant Amount	Partner Amount	Total Amount	Date Approved
Big Hill & Second Pond Forest Reserve	ME	P, O	$75,000	$505,000	$580,000	6/14/2006
Blaisdell - Clough I on the York River	ME	P	$30,000	$241,200	$271,200	6/21/2005
Caribou Bog/Katahdin Iron Works	ME	P	$75,000	$473,000	$548,000	6/14/2006
Conserving a Network of Wetlands in the Tatnics: Tatnic Woods III	ME	P	$50,000	$211,000	$261,000	6/21/2005
Greater Pleasant Bay Project Area II	ME	P	$950,000	$1,942,000	$2,892,000	9/13/2006
Greater York River Project Area	ME	P	$1,000,000	$2,380,200	$3,380,200	9/21/2005
Kennebec Estuary, Maine Phase II	ME	P, O	$1,000,000	$2,254,100	$3,254,100	9/13/2006
Machias River Project	ME	P	$1,000,000	$9,100,000	$10,100,000	9/21/2005
Northeast Penjajawoc Property Acquisition	ME	P	$75,000	$147,246	$222,246	6/14/2006
Northern Corea Heath Acquisition	ME	P	$75,000	$311,000	$386,000	6/14/2006
Richardson Seal Cove Property Acquisition	ME	P	$50,000	$700,000	$750,000	6/21/2005
Sucker Brook Project	ME	P	$75,000	$494,800	$569,800	6/14/2006
Upper Saco River Project: Hancock I	ME	P	$50,000	$105,000	$155,000	6/21/2005
Total			**$4,505,000**	**$18,864,546**	**$23,369,546**	
Gateway To The Jordan River	MI	P	$75,000	$622,800	$697,800	6/13/2007
Nayanquing Point SWA Coastal Wetland & Grassland	MI	H, O	$36,105	$191,630	$227,735	6/21/2005
Saginaw Bay to Lake Erie Coastal Habitat Project	MI	P, H, O	$1,000,000	$2,467,352	$3,467,352	9/21/2005
Saint Clair Lake/Six Mile Lake Natural Area Addition	MI	P	$75,000	$75,000	$150,000	6/13/2007
Wetland Property Acquisition for Migratory Birds	MI	P, O	$50,000	$61,800	$111,800	6/21/2005
Wigwam Bay SWA Coastal Wetland Restoration	MI	H, O	$75,000	$77,000	$152,000	6/14/2006
Total			**$1,311,105**	**$3,495,582**	**$4,806,687**	
Border Prairie Wetlands	MN	P, H, O	$1,000,000	$2,222,345	$3,222,345	9/13/2006
Carlos Avery WMA Wetland Enhancements	MN	H, O	$75,000	$299,425	$374,425	6/14/2006
Geneva Lake Conservation Easements	MN	P, O	$75,000	$301,241	$376,241	6/14/2006
Lower Minnesota Prairie Coteau	MN	P, H, O	$75,000	$82,000	$157,000	6/14/2006
Lower Minnesota Valley Wetland Conservation	MN	P, H, O	$1,000,000	$2,155,647	$3,155,647	3/8/2006
Minnesota Headwaters I	MN	P, H, O	$1,000,000	$2,916,732	$3,916,732	9/13/2006
Rapids Lake Acquisition & Restoration Project	MN	P, H	$50,000	$79,741	$129,741	6/21/2005
Roberts Waterfowl Production Area Restoration	MN	P, H	$50,000	$365,700	$415,700	6/21/2005
Upper Minnesota River Valley Phase I	MN	P, H, O	$1,000,000	$2,306,397	$3,306,397	3/14/2007
Total			**$4,325,000**	**$10,729,228**	**$15,054,228**	
Lewis & Clark Floodplain Heritage Partnership III	MO	P, H	$1,000,000	$5,294,850	$6,294,850	9/13/2006
Montrose Wetland Restoration Partnership	MO	H, O	$75,000	$245,000	$320,000	6/13/2007
Total			**$1,075,000**	**$5,539,850**	**$6,614,850**	
Lower Mississippi Valley Ecosystem IV	MS, AR, LA	P, H, O	$1,000,000	$2,442,615	$3,442,615	9/13/2006
Malmaison WMA Forested Wetlands Enhancement	MS	P, H, O	$591,646	$1,417,081	$2,008,727	9/13/2006
Private Lands in the Lower Mississippi Valley & Gulf Coastal Plain II	MS, AR, LA	P, H	$495,000	$5,729,797	$6,224,797	9/21/2005
Total			**$2,086,646**	**$9,589,493**	**$11,676,139**	
Carter Ponds Restoration & Enhancement Project	MT	H, O	$75,000	$262,406	$337,406	6/14/2006
Lower Clark Fork River/Lake Pend Oreille Watershed	MT, ID	P, H, O	$1,000,000	$7,518,200	$8,518,200	3/14/2007
Madison/Gallatin Wetlands Conservation Project I	MT	P, H	$1,000,000	$14,467,805	$15,467,805	3/8/2006
Madison/Gallatin Wetlands Conservation Project II	MT	P, H	$1,000,000	$6,260,998	$7,260,998	3/14/2007
The Bitterroot Wetland Conservation Corridor	MT	P, H, O	$75,000	$309,201	$384,201	6/14/2006
Total			**$3,150,000**	**$28,818,610**	**$31,968,610**	

Multistate projects are listed in each state/territory where they occur. Full figures are given with each listing.

31

U.S. North American Wetlands Conservation Act Projects Arrayed by State
Federal and Partner Dollars Invested in Fiscal Years 2006-2007
[Section 10(2)]

Project Title	State/ Territory	Project Type	Grant Amount	Partner Amount	Total Amount	Date Approved
Butner - Falls of Neuse Game Land Managed Wetlands Enhancement Project	NC	H	$50,000	$50,000	$100,000	6/21/2005
Invasive Species Eradication & Habitat Revitalization: Orton Plantation	NC	H	$75,000	$75,000	$150,000	6/13/2007
North Carolina Onslow Bight Partnership II	NC	P, H, O	$1,000,000	$3,164,000	$4,164,000	9/21/2005
Roanoke River Migratory Bird Initiative II	NC, VA	P, H, O	$999,920	$2,795,686	$3,795,606	3/8/2006
Sound Investment Phase II	NC, VA	P, H, O	$1,000,000	$2,281,633	$3,281,633	9/21/2005
Suggs Millpond Game Land Managed Wetlands Enhancement Project	NC	P, H	$28,000	$80,052	$108,052	6/21/2005
Total			**$3,152,920**	**$8,446,371**	**$11,599,291**	
Chase Lake Area Wetland Project VII	ND	P, H, O	$1,000,000	$1,115,355	$2,115,355	9/13/2006
Missouri Coteau Habitat Conservation Project IV	ND	P, O	$1,000,000	$1,112,430	$2,112,430	9/21/2005
Missouri Coteau Habitat Conservation Project V	ND	P, O	$1,000,000	$1,126,689	$2,126,689	9/13/2006
Mouse River Watershed Enhancement Project V	ND	P, H, O	$510,000	$687,391	$1,197,391	3/8/2006
North Dakota Drift Prairie Project I	ND	P, H, O	$1,000,000	$1,098,773	$2,098,773	9/13/2006
North Dakota Great Plains Project V	ND	P, H, O	$1,000,000	$1,190,694	$2,190,694	3/14/2007
Northern Coteau Project V	ND	P, H, O	$1,000,000	$1,098,197	$2,098,197	9/21/2005
Total			**$6,510,000**	**$7,429,529**	**$13,939,529**	
Big Bend Reach of the Platte River Phase I	NE	P, H, O	$1,000,000	$1,851,441	$2,851,441	3/14/2007
Middle Missouri River II	NE, IA	P, H, O	$1,000,000	$2,530,933	$3,530,933	3/8/2006
Rainwater Basin Habitat Conservation Project II	NE	P, H, O	$1,000,000	$1,130,925	$2,130,925	3/14/2007
Total			**$3,000,000**	**$5,513,299**	**$8,513,299**	
Great Bay Estuary VI: Piscassic River Watershed	NH	P, O	$1,000,000	$5,474,257	$6,474,257	3/14/2007
Piscassic Greenway Conservation Initiative	NH	P	$50,000	$8,522,908	$8,572,908	6/21/2005
Robb Reservoir Landscape Conservation Project	NH	P	$75,000	$3,825,000	$3,900,000	6/14/2006
Wapack Wilderness Conservation Campaign	NH	P	$75,000	$2,010,000	$2,085,000	6/13/2007
Total			**$1,200,000**	**$19,832,165**	**$21,032,165**	
Ruby Lake NWR Wetland Enhancement	NV	H	$50,000	$594,760	$644,760	6/21/2005
Total			**$50,000**	**$594,760**	**$644,760**	
Acquisition & Protection of Private Property within Wetland Complex	NY	P, H, O	$16,400	$35,500	$51,900	6/21/2005
Saint Lawrence River Valley I	NY	P, H, O	$979,224	$5,142,318	$6,121,542	9/21/2005
Total			**$995,624**	**$5,177,818**	**$6,173,442**	
Abraham Marsh Wetland Enhancement Project	OH	H, O	$60,000	$60,000	$120,000	6/14/2006
Ohio Grand River Wetlands Project	OH	P, H, O	$1,000,000	$2,005,064	$3,005,064	9/21/2005
Total			**$1,060,000**	**$2,065,064**	**$3,125,064**	
Shaffer Playa, Oklahoma	OK	P, O	$75,000	$76,320	$151,320	6/14/2006
Total			**$75,000**	**$76,320**	**$151,320**	

Multistate projects are listed in each state/territory where they occur. Full figures are given with each listing.

U.S. North American Wetlands Conservation Act Projects Arrayed by State
Federal and Partner Dollars Invested in Fiscal Years 2006-2007
[Section 10(2)]

Project Title	State/ Territory	Project Type	Grant Amount	Partner Amount	Total Amount	Date Approved
Lake County Closed Basin Project II	OR	H, O	$1,000,000	$2,145,493	$3,145,493	9/13/2006
Lower Columbia River Ecoregion IV	OR, WA	P, H, O	$1,000,000	$3,510,033	$4,510,033	3/8/2006
Lower Columbia River Estuary Project II	OR, WA	P, H	$1,000,000	$2,213,082	$3,213,082	9/21/2005
Lower Yaquina Salt Marsh Conservation Project	OR	P, O	$45,000	$46,800	$91,800	6/14/2006
Restoration & Enhancement at Oaks Bottom Wildlife Refuge Phase I	OR	H, O	$75,000	$319,508	$394,508	6/13/2007
Upper Klamath Lakes Wetlands	OR	P, H, O	$1,000,000	$15,838,033	$16,838,033	9/13/2006
Upper Willamette Wetlands Conservation Initiative II	OR	P, H	$1,000,000	$3,988,683	$4,988,683	3/14/2007
Willamette River Delta Restoration Phase I	OR	P, H, O	$880,500	$2,079,588	$2,960,088	3/14/2007
Total			**$6,000,500**	**$30,141,220**	**$36,141,720**	
Buzzards Bay Watershed: Tiverton Great Swamp	RI	P, O	$300,000	$1,500,000	$1,800,000	9/13/2006
Wetland Restoration on Three NWR & Adjacent Land	RI	H, O	$50,000	$108,438	$158,438	6/21/2005
Total			**$350,000**	**$1,608,438**	**$1,958,438**	
Ace Basin: Edisto River Corridor Protection Project II	SC	P, O	$1,000,000	$5,124,325	$6,124,325	9/21/2005
Bear Island Club, Inc. Wetlands Restoration Project	SC	H	$74,600	$218,434	$293,034	6/13/2007
Cedar Island Enhancement Project	SC	H	$50,000	$53,000	$103,000	6/21/2005
Combahee Fields Revitalization Project	SC	H	$20,000	$30,000	$50,000	6/21/2005
Murphy Island Enhancement Project	SC	H	$50,000	$83,000	$133,000	6/21/2005
Santee NWR Cuddo Unit Project	SC	H	$4,500	$8,500	$13,000	6/14/2006
South Carolina Pee Dee River Conservation Initiative: Woodbury Tract	SC	P	$1,000,000	$27,200,000	$28,200,000	9/13/2006
South Carolina Savannah River Conservation Initiative: Hamilton Ridge Tract	SC	P	$1,000,000	$22,200,000	$23,200,000	9/13/2006
Total			**$3,199,100**	**$54,917,259**	**$58,116,359**	
James River Lowlands/Missouri Coteau Project II	SD	P, O	$1,000,000	$1,851,391	$2,851,391	3/8/2006
James River Lowlands/Missouri Coteau Project III	SD	P, O	$1,000,000	$1,187,225	$2,187,225	3/14/2007
Total			**$2,000,000**	**$3,038,616**	**$5,038,616**	
Big Swan Headwaters Preserve: Boiling Springs Tract	TN	P, H	$25,000	$25,415	$50,415	6/13/2007
Lower Obion River III	TN	P, H, O	$1,000,000	$3,406,863	$4,406,863	3/8/2006
Restoration of Lick Creek Wetlands - Joachim Bible Refuge Tracts	TN	P, H	$75,000	$937,415	$1,012,415	6/14/2006
Wolf River, Tennessee Phase II	TN	P, H	$1,000,000	$12,011,076	$13,011,076	3/14/2007
Total			**$2,100,000**	**$16,380,769**	**$18,480,769**	
Austins Woods III	TX	P	$586,000	$894,539	$1,480,539	3/14/2007
Chenier Plain Coastal Wetlands Conservation IV	TX, LA	P, H, O	$637,771	$1,593,624	$2,231,395	3/8/2006
Chenier Plain Coastal Wetlands Conservation V	TX, LA	P, O	$1,000,000	$3,005,040	$4,005,040	9/13/2006
Coastal Prairie Wetlands Restoration & Acquisition	TX	P, H	$1,000,000	$2,598,280	$3,598,280	9/21/2005
Gulf Coast JV Mottled Duck Conservation Plan	TX	P, H	$67,500	$103,000	$170,500	6/13/2007
Lower Neches River Cypress	TX, LA	P, O	$932,200	$3,104,640	$4,036,840	3/14/2007
Mud Flats Pass Culvert Project	TX	H	$31,000	$46,380	$77,380	6/14/2006
Rio Bosque Water Supply Well	TX	H	$9,000	$45,818	$54,818	6/21/2005
Wetland Enhancement for the Myrtle Foester - Whitmire Preserve	TX	H	$37,228	$43,944	$81,172	6/21/2005
Wetland Restoration & Enhancement of Private & Public Lands of the Texas Gulf Coast V	TX	H, O	$969,141	$2,332,767	$3,301,908	3/14/2007
Total			**$5,269,840**	**$13,768,032**	**$19,037,872**	

Multistate projects are listed in each state/territory where they occur. Full figures are given with each listing.

33

U.S. North American Wetlands Conservation Act Projects Arrayed by State
Federal and Partner Dollars Invested in Fiscal Years 2006-2007
[Section 10(2)]

Project Title	State/ Territory	Project Type	Grant Amount	Partner Amount	Total Amount	Date Approved
The New State Wetland Enhancement	UT	H	$49,112	$131,923	$181,035	6/21/2005
Total			**$49,112**	**$131,923**	**$181,035**	
Allegheny Mountain - Northern Ridge & Valley	VA, WV, MD	H, O	$75,000	$215,589	$290,589	6/13/2007
Lower Rappahannock Phase III	VA	P	$700,000	$4,508,200	$5,208,200	3/8/2006
Roanoke River Migratory Bird Initiative II	VA, NC	P, H, O	$999,920	$2,795,686	$3,795,606	3/8/2006
Sound Investment Phase II	VA, NC	P, H, O	$1,000,000	$2,281,633	$3,281,633	9/21/2005
Southern Tip Cooperative Conservation Initiative	VA	P, H	$1,000,000	$14,134,000	$15,134,000	9/13/2006
Total			**$3,774,920**	**$23,935,108**	**$27,710,028**	
Bagley Lake Farm Wetland Restoration, Olympic Peninsula	WA	H, O	$15,918	$17,194	$33,112	6/21/2005
Chehalis River Floodplain & Estuary Wetland Conservation	WA	P, H, O	$988,425	$7,628,000	$8,616,425	3/8/2006
Crow Marsh Project - Crow Marsh East	WA	P, H, O	$30,000	$30,000	$60,000	6/13/2007
Lower Columbia River Ecoregion IV	WA, OR	P, H, O	$1,000,000	$3,510,033	$4,510,033	3/8/2006
Lower Columbia River Estuary Project II	WA, OR	P, H	$1,000,000	$2,213,082	$3,213,082	9/21/2005
Lower Yakima Wetlands Protection/Restoration II	WA	P, H, O	$1,000,000	$3,201,395	$4,201,395	9/13/2006
Lummi Island Conservation Project	WA	P	$75,000	$3,344,500	$3,419,500	6/14/2006
Middle Puget Sound Wetlands Phase I	WA	P, H, O	$1,000,000	$2,333,459	$3,333,459	9/21/2005
North Willapa Bay Wetlands Conservation	WA	P, H, O	$1,000,000	$2,119,500	$3,119,500	9/13/2006
Otto Preserve Expansion Project	WA	P, O	$50,000	$340,000	$390,000	6/21/2005
Total			**$6,159,343**	**$24,737,163**	**$30,896,506**	
Hawk Metals Wetland Acquisition	WI	P	$50,000	$200,000	$250,000	6/14/2006
Leopold Memorial Reserve - Migratory Habitat Expansion	WI	P, H, O	$50,000	$91,550	$141,550	6/21/2005
Lower Chippewa River Wetland Protection Partnership II	WI	P, H, O	$1,000,000	$3,110,010	$4,110,010	3/8/2006
Scuppernong River Wetland Restoration Phase II	WI	H	$50,000	$90,000	$140,000	6/21/2005
Southcentral Wisconsin Prairie Pothole Initiative III	WI	P, H, O	$1,000,000	$3,147,235	$4,147,235	9/21/2005
The Des Plaines River Lowlands Conservation Project	WI	P, H, O	$75,000	$259,500	$334,500	6/13/2007
Whitefish Lake & Wetland Preservation	WI	P	$50,000	$726,500	$776,500	6/21/2005
Willow River & Kinnickinnic State Parks Nesting Habitat Enhancement	WI	H, O	$50,000	$96,075	$146,075	6/21/2005
Wisconsin Private Lands Conservation: 10 Projects in Southern Wisconsin	WI	H	$12,000	$12,697	$24,697	6/21/2005
Total			**$2,337,000**	**$7,733,567**	**$10,070,567**	
Allegheny Mountain - Northern Ridge & Valley	WV, MD, VA	H, O	$75,000	$215,589	$290,589	6/13/2007
Total			**$75,000**	**$215,589**	**$290,589**	

Multistate projects are listed in each state/territory where they occur. Full figures are given with each listing.

Canadian North American Wetlands Conservation Act Projects Arrayed by Province
Federal and Partner Dollars Invested in Fiscal Years 2006-2007
[Section 10(2)]

Project Title	Province/ Territory	Project Type	Grant Amount	Partner Amount	Total Amount	Date Approved
Alberta Habitat Program	AB, BC	P, H, O	$1,020,072	$1,567,072	$2,587,144	9/21/2005
Canadian Intermountain JV & Pacific Coast JV Wetland - Associated Migratory Bird Habitat	AB, BC	P, H, O	$172,500	$692,500	$865,000	9/21/2005
Canadian Intermountain JV & Pacific Coast JV Wetland - Associated Migratory Bird Habitat	AB, BC	P, H, O	$296,612	$673,388	$970,000	6/14/2006
Canadian Intermountain JV & Pacific Coast JV	AB, BC	P, H, O	$550,000	$1,180,000	$1,730,000	6/13/2007
Critical Wetland & Upland Habitat - Alberta	AB	P, H, O	$420,000	$1,192,000	$1,612,000	9/21/2005
Potholes Plus Project	AB, MB	P, H, O	$491,300	$984,100	$1,475,400	9/21/2005
Potholes Plus Project	AB, MB, SK	P, H, O	$500,000	$1,005,000	$1,505,000	6/13/2007
Prairie - Western Boreal Region Habitat Program	AB, BC, MB, NT, SK, YT	P, H, O	$11,505,693	$14,650,693	$26,156,386	6/14/2006
Prairie - Western Boreal Region Habitat Program	AB, BC, MB, NT, SK, YT	P, H, O	$3,942,000	$4,922,000	$8,864,000	9/13/2006
Prairie - Western Boreal Region Habitat Program	AB, BC, MB, NT, SK, YT	P, H, O	$10,839,938	$13,641,938	$24,481,876	6/13/2007
Prairie Canada Wetlands & Uplands	AB, SK	P, H, O	$1,508,436	$2,578,436	$4,086,872	6/14/2006
Prairie Canada Wetlands & Uplands	AB, MB, SK	P, H, O	$1,950,000	$3,257,000	$5,207,000	6/13/2007
Total			**$33,196,551**	**$46,344,127**	**$79,540,678**	
Alberta Habitat Program	BC, AB	P, H, O	$1,020,072	$1,567,072	$2,587,144	9/21/2005
Canadian Intermountain JV & Pacific Coast JV Wetland - Associated Migratory Bird Habitat	BC, AB	P, H, O	$172,500	$692,500	$865,000	9/21/2005
Canadian Intermountain JV & Pacific Coast JV Wetland - Associated Migratory Bird Habitat	BC, AB	P, H, O	$296,612	$673,388	$970,000	6/14/2006
Canadian Intermountain JV & Pacific Coast JV Wetland - Associated Migratory Bird Habitat	BC, AB	P, H, O	$550,000	$1,180,000	$1,730,000	6/13/2007
Critical Wetlands & Associated Upland Habitats	BC	P, H, O	$294,128	$969,128	$1,263,256	9/21/2005
Critical Wetlands & Associated Upland Habitats	BC	P, H, O	$1,527,231	$2,569,231	$4,096,462	6/14/2006
Critical Wetlands & Associated Upland Habitats	BC	P, H, O	$540,000	$1,010,000	$1,550,000	9/13/2006
Critical Wetlands & Associated Upland Habitats	BC	P, H, O	$1,321,250	$2,336,250	$3,657,500	6/13/2007
Prairie - Western Boreal Region Habitat Program	BC, AB, MB, NT, SK, YT	P, H, O	$11,505,693	$14,650,693	$26,156,386	6/14/2006
Prairie - Western Boreal Region Habitat Program	BC, AB, MB, NT, SK, YT	P, H, O	$3,942,000	$4,922,000	$8,864,000	9/13/2006
Prairie - Western Boreal Region Habitat Program	BC, AB, MB, NT, SK, YT	P, H, O	$10,839,938	$13,641,938	$24,481,876	6/13/2007
Total			**$32,009,424**	**$44,212,200**	**$76,221,624**	
Manitoba Critical Wetland & Upland Habitat	MB	P, H, O	$192,124	$337,124	$529,248	9/21/2005
Potholes Plus Project	MB, AB	P, H, O	$491,300	$984,100	$1,475,400	9/21/2005
Potholes Plus Project	MB, AB, SK	P, H, O	$500,000	$1,005,000	$1,505,000	6/13/2007
Prairie - Western Boreal Region Habitat Program	MB, AB, BC, NT, SK, YT	P, H, O	$11,505,693	$14,650,693	$26,156,386	6/14/2006
Prairie - Western Boreal Region Habitat Program	MB, AB, BC, NT, SK, YT	P, H, O	$3,942,000	$4,922,000	$8,864,000	9/13/2006
Prairie - Western Boreal Region Habitat Program	MB, AB, BC, NT, SK, YT	P, H, O	$10,839,938	$13,641,938	$24,481,876	6/13/2007
Prairie Canada Wetlands & Uplands	MB, AB, SK	P, H, O	$1,950,000	$3,257,000	$5,207,000	6/13/2007
Total			**$29,421,055**	**$38,797,855**	**$68,218,910**	

Multistate projects are listed in each province/territory where they occur. Full figures are given with each listing.

Canadian North American Wetlands Conservation Act Projects Arrayed by Province
Federal and Partner Dollars Invested in Fiscal Years 2006-2007
[Section 10(2)]

Project Title	Province/ Territory	Project Type	Grant Amount	Partner Amount	Total Amount	Date Approved
Atlantic Canada Wetland Securement Project	NB, NF	P, H, O	$78,600	$105,600	$184,200	9/21/2005
Atlantic Canada Wetlands Conservation	NB, NF, NS	P, H, O	$150,400	$160,400	$310,800	9/21/2005
Atlantic Coastal Waterfowl Habitat Conservation	NB, PE	P, H, O	$300,000	$425,000	$725,000	6/13/2007
Eastern Habitat JV Wetlands Conservation	NB, NF, NS, ON, PE, QC	P, H, O	$2,531,068	$3,325,068	$5,856,136	6/14/2006
Eastern Habitat JV Wetlands Conservation	NB, NF, NS, ON, PE, QC	P, H, O	$854,250	$1,323,250	$2,177,500	9/13/2006
Eastern Habitat JV Wetlands Conservation	NB, NF, NS, ON, PE, QC	P, H, O	$2,246,149	$3,114,149	$5,360,298	6/13/2007
Maritimes Wetland Securement Project	NB, NS, PE	P, H, O	$258,814	$338,814	$597,628	6/14/2006
Total			**$6,419,281**	**$8,792,281**	**$15,211,562**	
Atlantic Canada Wetland Securement Project	NF, NB	P, H, O	$78,600	$105,600	$184,200	9/21/2005
Atlantic Canada Wetlands Conservation	NF, NB, NS	P, H, O	$150,400	$160,400	$310,800	9/21/2005
Eastern Habitat JV Wetlands Conservation	NF, NB, NS, ON, PE, QC	P, H, O	$2,531,068	$3,325,068	$5,856,136	6/14/2006
Eastern Habitat JV Wetlands Conservation	NF, NB, NS, ON, PE, QC	P, H, O	$854,250	$1,323,250	$2,177,500	9/13/2006
Eastern Habitat JV Wetlands Conservation	NF, NB, NS, ON, PE, QC	P, H, O	$2,246,149	$3,114,149	$5,360,298	6/13/2007
Total			**$5,860,467**	**$8,028,467**	**$13,888,934**	
Atlantic Canada Wetlands Conservation	NS, NB, NF	P, H, O	$150,400	$160,400	$310,800	9/21/2005
Eastern Habitat JV Wetlands Conservation	NS, NB, NF, ON, PE, QC	P, H, O	$2,531,068	$3,325,068	$5,856,136	6/14/2006
Eastern Habitat JV Wetlands Conservation	NS, NB, NF, ON, PE, QC	P, H, O	$854,250	$1,323,250	$2,177,500	9/13/2006
Eastern Habitat JV Wetlands Conservation	NS, NB, NF, ON, PE, QC	P, H, O	$2,246,149	$3,114,149	$5,360,298	6/13/2007
Maritimes Wetland Securement Project	NS, NB, PE	P, H, O	$258,814	$338,814	$597,628	6/14/2006
Total			**$6,040,681**	**$8,261,681**	**$14,302,362**	
Prairie - Western Boreal Region Habitat Program	NT, AB, BC, MB, SK, YT	P, H, O	$11,505,693	$14,650,693	$26,156,386	6/14/2006
Prairie - Western Boreal Region Habitat Program	NT, AB, BC, MB, SK, YT	P, H, O	$3,942,000	$4,922,000	$8,864,000	9/13/2006
Prairie - Western Boreal Region Habitat Program	NT, AB, BC, MB, SK, YT	P, H, O	$10,839,938	$13,641,938	$24,481,876	6/13/2007
Total			**$26,287,631**	**$33,214,631**	**$59,502,262**	
Ducks Unlimited Canada Ontario Project	ON	P, H, O	$137,000	$167,000	$304,000	9/21/2005
Eastern Habitat JV Wetlands Conservation	ON, NB, NF, NS, PE, QC	P, H, O	$2,531,068	$3,325,068	$5,856,136	6/14/2006
Eastern Habitat JV Wetlands Conservation	ON, NB, NF, NS, PE, QC	P, H, O	$854,250	$1,323,250	$2,177,500	9/13/2006
Eastern Habitat JV Wetlands Conservation	ON, NB, NF, NS, PE, QC	P, H, O	$2,246,149	$3,114,149	$5,360,298	6/13/2007
Great Lakes Wetlands Habitat Conservation Project	ON	P, H, O	$127,500	$327,500	$455,000	9/21/2005
Ontario Wetland Habitat Fund Program	ON	P, H, O	$150,436	$903,436	$1,053,872	9/21/2005
Total			**$6,046,403**	**$9,160,403**	**$15,206,806**	

Multistate projects are listed in each province/territory where they occur. Full figures are given with each listing.

Canadian North American Wetlands Conservation Act Projects Arrayed by Province
Federal and Partner Dollars Invested in Fiscal Years 2006-2007
[Section 10(2)]

Project Title	Province/ Territory	Project Type	Grant Amount	Partner Amount	Total Amount	Date Approved
Atlantic Coastal Waterfowl Habitat Conservation	PE, NB	P, H, O	$300,000	$425,000	$725,000	6/13/2007
Eastern Habitat JV Wetlands Conservation	PE, NB, NF, NS, ON, QC	P, H, O	$2,531,068	$3,325,068	$5,856,136	6/14/2006
Eastern Habitat JV Wetlands Conservation	PE, NB, NF, NS, ON, QC	P, H, O	$854,250	$1,323,250	$2,177,500	9/13/2006
Eastern Habitat JV Wetlands Conservation	PE, NB, NF, NS, ON, QC	P, H, O	$2,246,149	$3,114,149	$5,360,298	6/13/2007
Maritimes Wetland Securement Project	PE, NB, NS	P, H, O	$258,814	$338,814	$597,628	6/14/2006
Total			**$6,190,281**	**$8,526,281**	**$14,716,562**	
Eastern Habitat JV Wetlands Conservation	QC, NB, NF, NS, ON, PE	P, H, O	$2,531,068	$3,325,068	$5,856,136	6/14/2006
Eastern Habitat JV Wetlands Conservation	QC, NB, NF, NS, ON, PE	P, H, O	$854,250	$1,323,250	$2,177,500	9/13/2006
Eastern Habitat JV Wetlands Conservation	QC, NB, NF, NS, ON, PE	P, H, O	$2,246,149	$3,114,149	$5,360,298	6/13/2007
Quebec: Protecting Wetland & Upland Habitat	QC	P, H, O	$223,280	$379,280	$602,560	6/14/2006
Quebec: Protecting Wetland & Upland Habitat	QC	P, H, O	$63,750	$259,495	$323,245	9/13/2006
Quebec: Protecting Wetland & Upland Habitat	QC	P, H, O	$250,000	$550,000	$800,000	6/13/2007
Quebec/Saint Lawrence Watershed	QC	P, H, O	$143,718	$243,718	$387,436	9/21/2005
Saint Lawrence River & Lake Champlain Critical Wetland Habitat Project	QC	P, H, O	$63,750	$263,750	$327,500	9/21/2005
Total			**$6,375,965**	**$9,458,710**	**$15,834,675**	
Potholes Plus Project	SK, AB, MB	P, H, O	$500,000	$1,005,000	$1,505,000	6/13/2007
Prairie - Western Boreal Region Habitat Program	SK, AB, BC, MB, NT, YT	P, H, O	$11,505,693	$14,650,693	$26,156,386	6/14/2006
Prairie - Western Boreal Region Habitat Program	SK, AB, BC, MB, NT, YT	P, H, O	$3,942,000	$4,922,000	$8,864,000	9/13/2006
Prairie - Western Boreal Region Habitat Program	SK, AB, BC, MB, NT, YT	P, H, O	$10,839,938	$13,641,938	$24,481,876	6/13/2007
Prairie Canada Wetlands & Uplands	SK, AB	P, H, O	$1,508,436	$2,578,436	$4,086,872	6/14/2006
Prairie Canada Wetlands & Uplands	SK, AB, MB	P, H, O	$1,950,000	$3,257,000	$5,207,000	6/13/2007
Saskatchewan Habitat Program	SK	P, H, O	$1,020,072	$1,165,072	$2,185,144	9/21/2005
Saskatchewan Wetlands & Uplands	SK	P, H, O	$420,000	$800,000	$1,220,000	9/21/2005
Total			**$31,686,139**	**$42,020,139**	**$73,706,278**	
Prairie - Western Boreal Region Habitat Program	YT, AB, BC, MB, NT, SK	P, H, O	$11,505,693	$14,650,693	$26,156,386	6/14/2006
Prairie - Western Boreal Region Habitat Program	YT, AB, BC, MB, NT, SK	P, H, O	$3,942,000	$4,922,000	$8,864,000	9/13/2006
Prairie - Western Boreal Region Habitat Program	YT, AB, BC, MB, NT, SK	P, H, O	$10,839,938	$13,641,938	$24,481,876	6/13/2007
Total			**$26,287,631**	**$33,214,631**	**$59,502,262**	

Multistate projects are listed in each province/territory where they occur. Full figures are given with each listing.

Mexican North American Wetlands Conservation Act Projects Arrayed by State
Federal and Partner Dollars Invested in Fiscal Years 2006-2007
[Section 10(2)]

Project Title	State	Project Type	Grant Amount	Partner Amount	Total Amount	Date Approved
Inventory & Classification of Critical Wetlands V: Central Highlands	AGS/*1	O	$306,979	$309,737	$616,716	3/8/2006
Total			**$306,979**	**$309,737**	**$616,716**	
Bahia San Quintin: Protecting & Managing a Critical Wetland for Pacific Brant	BCN	O	$100,168	$114,500	$214,668	3/8/2006
Conservation in a Maritime Zone in Bahia San Quintin	BCN	O	$99,598	$100,750	$200,348	3/8/2006
Conservation of Brant & Other Migratory Waterbirds, Guerrero Negro - Ojo De Liebre Lagoon	BCN, BCS	O	$251,115	$371,704	$622,819	3/8/2006
Development of A Monitoring Protocol & a Systematized Survey System	BCN/*2	O	$50,433	$50,457	$100,890	3/14/2007
Joint Initiative for the Restoration of the Colorado River Delta	BCN, SON	H, O	$293,675	$310,311	$603,986	3/8/2006
Strengthening the National Shorebird Plan thru Development & Distribution of Outreach	BCN,/*2,	O	$14,620	$15,845	$30,465	3/8/2006
The 2008-2009 Veracruz Model	BCN, SIN, SON	O	$145,000	$156,008	$301,008	3/14/2007
Total			**$954,609**	**$1,119,575**	**$2,074,184**	
Conservation of Brant & Other Migratory Waterbirds, Guerrero Negro - Ojo De Liebre Lagoon	BCS, BCN	O	$251,115	$371,704	$622,819	3/8/2006
Conservation of the Brant (Branta Bernicla) in San Ignacio Lagoon	BCS	O	$247,296	$275,506	$522,802	3/14/2007
Development of A Monitoring Protocol & a Systematized Survey System	BCS/*2	O	$50,433	$50,457	$100,890	3/14/2007
Implementation of Legal Conservation Mechanisms in Laguna San Ignacio II	BCS	P	$407,538	$1,230,369	$1,637,907	3/14/2007
Management & Protection of the Wintering Habitat of the Pacific Brant In Bahia Magdalena	BCS	O	$76,154	$96,845	$172,999	3/8/2006
Strengthening the National Shorebird Plan thru Development & Distribution of Outreach	BCS/*2	O	$14,620	$15,845	$30,465	3/8/2006
Total			**$1,047,156**	**$2,040,726**	**$3,087,882**	
Development of A Monitoring Protocol & a Systematized Survey System	CAM/*2	O	$50,433	$50,457	$100,890	3/14/2007
Strengthening the National Shorebird Plan thru Development & Distribution of Outreach	CAM/*2	O	$14,620	$15,845	$30,465	3/8/2006
Total			**$65,053**	**$66,302**	**$131,355**	
Development of a Watershed Management Plan - Mexicanos Lagoon	CHIH	O	$40,021	$40,024	$80,045	3/8/2006
Waterfowl Reserve Network in Northwest Chihuahua	CHIH	P, H, O	$234,040	$271,240	$505,280	3/8/2006
Total			**$274,061**	**$311,264**	**$585,325**	

Multistate projects are listed in each state where they occur. Full figures are given with each listing.

1 - AGS, COL, D.F., GTO, JAL, MEX, MICH, MOR, NAY, PUE, QRO, SLP, TLAX, ZAC

2 - BCN, BCS, CAM, CHIS, JAL, MEX, MICH, NAY, Q.ROO, SIN, SON, TAB, TAMPS, VER, YUC

Mexican North American Wetlands Conservation Act Projects Arrayed by State
Federal and Partner Dollars Invested in Fiscal Years 2006-2007
[Section 10(2)]

Project Title	State	Project Type	Grant Amount	Partner Amount	Total Amount	Date Approved
Development of A Monitoring Protocol & a Systematized Survey System	CHIS/*2	O	$50,433	$50,457	$100,890	3/14/2007
Protection, Management & Rehabilation of Lajoya - Buenavista & Manguito - Chocohuital Wetlands	CHIS	P, H	$127,034	$128,000	$255,034	3/14/2007
Strengthening the National Shorebird Plan thru Development & Distribution of Outreach	CHIS/*2	O	$14,620	$15,845	$30,465	3/8/2006
Total			**$192,087**	**$194,302**	**$386,389**	
Waterfowl Refuges in Cuatrocienegas, Coahuila	COAH	P, H	$159,600	$273,760	$433,360	3/8/2006
Total			**$159,600**	**$273,760**	**$433,360**	
Inventory & Classification of Critical Wetlands V: Central Highlands	COL/*1	O	$306,979	$309,737	$616,716	3/8/2006
Total			**$306,979**	**$309,737**	**$616,716**	
Inventory & Classification of Critical Wetlands V: Central Highlands	D.F./*1	O	$306,979	$309,737	$616,716	3/8/2006
Total			**$306,979**	**$309,737**	**$616,716**	
Wetland Restoration & Public Outreach Program for the Conservation of the Malaga Wetlands	DGO	H, O	$115,513	$221,370	$336,883	3/14/2007
Total			**$115,513**	**$221,370**	**$336,883**	
Inventory & Classification of Critical Wetlands V: Central Highlands	D.F./*1	O	$306,979	$309,737	$616,716	3/8/2006
Participatory Planning for Sustainable Management of Lake Cuitzeo	GTO, MICH	O	$91,654	$91,684	$183,338	3/14/2007
Social & Public Outreach Program for Conservation & Sustainable Use of Yuriria Lagoon	GTO	O	$57,732	$148,266	$205,998	3/8/2006
Total			**$456,365**	**$549,687**	**$1,006,052**	
Development of A Monitoring Protocol & a Systematized Survey System	JAL/*2	O	$50,433	$50,457	$100,890	3/14/2007
Development of a Conservation & Envirnmental Education Program for Sayula Lagoon	JAL	O	$130,184	$151,875	$282,059	3/14/2007
Ecotourism & Restoration of Habitat at Laguna Sayula II	JAL	H, O	$98,746	$272,376	$371,122	3/8/2006
Inventory & Classification of Critical Wetlands V: Central Highlands	JAL/*1	O	$306,979	$309,737	$616,716	3/8/2006
Strengthening the National Shorebird Plan thru Development & Distribution of Outreach	JAL/*2	O	$14,620	$15,845	$30,465	3/8/2006
Total			**$600,962**	**$800,290**	**$1,401,252**	

Multistate projects are listed in each state where they occur. Full figures are given with each listing.
1 - AGS, COL, D.F., GTO, JAL, MEX, MICH, MOR, NAY, PUE, QRO, SLP, TLAX, ZAC
2 - BCN, BCS, CAM, CHIS, JAL, MEX, MICH, NAY, Q.ROO, SIN, SON, TAB, TAMPS, VER, YUC

Mexican North American Wetlands Conservation Act Projects Arrayed by State
Federal and Partner Dollars Invested in Fiscal Years 2006-2007
[Section 10(2)]

Project Title	State	Project Type	Grant Amount	Partner Amount	Total Amount	Date Approved
Development of A Monitoring Protocol & a Systematized Survey System	MEX/*2	O	$50,433	$50,457	$100,890	3/14/2007
Inventory & Classification of Critical Wetlands V: Central Highlands	MEX/*1	O	$306,979	$309,737	$616,716	3/8/2006
Strengthening the National Shorebird Plan thru Development & Distribution of Outreach	MEX/*2	O	$14,620	$15,845	$30,465	3/8/2006
Total			**$372,032**	**$376,039**	**$748,071**	
Development of A Monitoring Protocol & a Systematized Survey System	MICH/*2	O	$50,433	$50,457	$100,890	3/14/2007
Inventory & Classification of Critical Wetlands V: Central Highlands	MICH/*1	O	$306,979	$309,737	$616,716	3/8/2006
Participatory Planning for Sustainable Management of Lake Cuitzeo	MICH, GTO	O	$91,654	$91,684	$183,338	3/14/2007
Strengthening the National Shorebird Plan thru Development & Distribution of Outreach	MICH/*2	O	$14,620	$15,845	$30,465	3/8/2006
Total			**$463,686**	**$467,723**	**$931,409**	
Inventory & Classification of Critical Wetlands V: Central Highlands	MOR/*1	O	$306,979	$309,737	$616,716	3/8/2006
Total			**$306,979**	**$309,737**	**$616,716**	
Development of A Monitoring Protocol & a Systematized Survey System	NAY/*2	O	$50,433	$50,457	$100,890	3/14/2007
Inventory & Classification of Critical Wetlands V: Central Highlands	NAY/*1	O	$306,979	$309,737	$616,716	3/8/2006
Strengthening the National Shorebird Plan thru Development & Distribution of Outreach	NAY/*2	O	$14,620	$15,845	$30,465	3/8/2006
Total			**$372,032**	**$376,039**	**$748,071**	
Inventory & Classification of Critical Wetlands V: Central Highlands	PUE/*1	O	$306,979	$309,737	$616,716	3/8/2006
Total			**$306,979**	**$309,737**	**$616,716**	
Development of A Monitoring Protocol & a Systematized Survey System	Q.ROO/*2	O	$50,433	$50,457	$100,890	3/14/2007
Strengthening the National Shorebird Plan thru Development & Distribution of Outreach	Q.ROO/*2	O	$14,620	$15,845	$30,465	3/8/2006
Total			**$65,053**	**$66,302**	**$131,355**	
Inventory & Classification of Critical Wetlands V: Central Highlands	QRO/*1	O	$306,979	$309,737	$616,716	3/8/2006
Total			**$306,979**	**$309,737**	**$616,716**	

Multistate projects are listed in each state where they occur. Full figures are given with each listing.
1 - AGS, COL, D.F., GTO, JAL, MEX, MICH, MOR, NAY, PUE, QRO, SLP, TLAX, ZAC
2 - BCN, BCS, CAM, CHIS, JAL, MEX, MICH, NAY, Q.ROO, SIN, SON, TAB, TAMPS, VER, YUC

Mexican North American Wetlands Conservation Act Projects Arrayed by State
Federal and Partner Dollars Invested in Fiscal Years 2006-2007
[Section 10(2)]

Project Title	State	Project Type	Grant Amount	Partner Amount	Total Amount	Date Approved
Conservation of Wintering Areas for Migratory Waterfowl & Shorebirds in Sonora & Sinaloa	SIN, SON	P, O	$206,000	$206,000	$412,000	3/14/2007
Development of A Monitoring Protocol & a Systematized Survey System	SIN/*2	O	$50,433	$50,457	$100,890	3/14/2007
Implementation of the Conservation & Management Plan for Huizache-Caimanero Lagoon II	SIN	O	$64,779	$75,438	$140,217	3/14/2007
Restoration Program for Critical Wetland Habitat in Ensenada De Pabellones II	SIN	H, O	$386,868	$875,416	$1,262,284	3/8/2006
Strengthening the National Shorebird Plan thru Development & Distribution of Outreach	SIN/*2	O	$14,620	$15,845	$30,465	3/8/2006
The 2008-2009 Veracruz Model	SIN, BCN, SON	O	$145,000	$156,008	$301,008	3/14/2007
Total			**$867,700**	**$1,379,164**	**$2,246,864**	
Inventory & Classification of Critical Wetlands V: Central Highlands	SLP/*1	O	$306,979	$309,737	$616,716	3/8/2006
Total			**$306,979**	**$309,737**	**$616,716**	
Conservation of Wintering Areas for Migratory Waterfowl & Shorebirds in Sonora & Sinaloa	SON, SIN	P, O	$206,000	$206,000	$412,000	3/14/2007
Development of A Monitoring Protocol & a Systematized Survey System	SON/*2	O	$50,433	$50,457	$100,890	3/14/2007
Joint Initiative for the Restoration of the Colorado River Delta	SON, BCN	H, O	$293,675	$310,311	$603,986	3/8/2006
Strengthening the National Shorebird Plan thru Development & Distribution of Outreach	SON/*2	O	$14,620	$15,845	$30,465	3/8/2006
The 2008-2009 Veracruz Model	SON, BCN, SIN	O	$145,000	$156,008	$301,008	3/14/2007
Total			**$709,728**	**$738,621**	**$1,448,349**	
Development of A Monitoring Protocol & a Systematized Survey System	TAB/*2	O	$50,433	$50,457	$100,890	3/14/2007
Environmental Education Workshops for Wetlands	TAB	O	$155,696	$362,300	$517,996	3/8/2006
Strengthening the National Shorebird Plan thru Development & Distribution of Outreach	TAB/*2	O	$14,620	$15,845	$30,465	3/8/2006
Total			**$220,749**	**$428,602**	**$649,351**	
Development of A Monitoring Protocol & a Systematized Survey System	TAMPS/*2	O	$50,433	$50,457	$100,890	3/14/2007
Lagoon Restoration in the Natural Protected Area of Laguna Madre	TAMPS	H, O	$147,224	$149,760	$296,984	3/8/2006
Protection of Sea Grasses for the Conservation of Waterfowl in Laguna Madre	TAMPS	P, O	$172,860	$174,760	$347,620	3/14/2007
Restoration of Wetlands & Land Purchase in the Rio Grande Delta	TAMPS	P, H	$732,710	$1,077,971	$1,810,681	3/14/2007
Restoration Planning & Monitoring of Wetlands for a Biological Corridor	TAMPS	O	$119,735	$149,489	$269,224	3/14/2007
Strengthening the National Shorebird Plan thru Development & Distribution of Outreach	TAMPS/*2	O	$14,620	$15,845	$30,465	3/8/2006
Total			**$1,237,582**	**$1,618,282**	**$2,855,864**	

Multistate projects are listed in each state where they occur. Full figures are given with each listing.
1 - AGS, COL, D.F., GTO, JAL, MEX, MICH, MOR, NAY, PUE, QRO, SLP, TLAX, ZAC
2 - BCN, BCS, CAM, CHIS, JAL, MEX, MICH, NAY, Q.ROO, SIN, SON, TAB, TAMPS, VER, YUC

41

Mexican North American Wetlands Conservation Act Projects Arrayed by State
Federal and Partner Dollars Invested in Fiscal Years 2006-2007
[Section 10(2)]

Project Title	State	Project Type	Grant Amount	Partner Amount	Total Amount	Date Approved
Inventory & Classification of Critical Wetlands V: Central Highlands	TLAX/*1	O	$306,979	$309,737	$616,716	3/8/2006
Total			$306,979	$309,737	$616,716	
Development of A Monitoring Protocol & a Systematized Survey System	VER/*2	O	$50,433	$50,457	$100,890	3/14/2007
Restoration & Planning for Migratory Bird Habitat Conservation in Tamiahua, Veracruz	VER	O	$108,169	$118,296	$226,465	3/8/2006
Strengthening the National Shorebird Plan thru Development & Distribution of Outreach	VER/*2	O	$14,620	$15,845	$30,465	3/8/2006
Total			$173,222	$184,598	$357,820	
Development of A Monitoring Protocol & a Systematized Survey System	YUC/*2	O	$50,433	$50,457	$100,890	3/14/2007
Strengthening the National Shorebird Plan thru Development & Distribution of Outreach	YUC/*2	O	$14,620	$15,845	$30,465	3/8/2006
Total			$65,053	$66,302	$131,355	
Inventory & Classification of Critical Wetlands V: Central Highlands	ZAC/*1	O	$306,979	$309,737	$616,716	3/8/2006
Total			$306,979	$309,737	$616,716	

Multistate projects are listed in each state where they occur. Full figures are given with each listing.
1 - AGS, COL, D.F., GTO, JAL, MEX, MICH, MOR, NAY, PUE, QRO, SLP, TLAX, ZAC
2 - BCN, BCS, CAM, CHIS, JAL, MEX, MICH, NAY, Q.ROO, SIN, SON, TAB, TAMPS, VER, YUC

North American Wetlands Conservation Act
The North American Wetlands Conservation Council

Duane Shroufe (Chair), Director, Arizona Game and Fish Department

Wayne MacCallum (Vice Chair), Director, Massachusetts Division of Fisheries and Wildlife

Dale Hall, Director, U.S. Fish and Wildlife Service

Scott Henderson, Director, Arkansas Game and Fish Commission

Mary Pope Hutson, Vice President, The Land Trust Alliance

David Nomsen, Vice President, Governmental Affairs, Pheasants Forever, Inc.

Terry Steinwand, Director, North Dakota Game & Fish Department

Jeff Trandahl, Executive Director, National Fish and Wildlife Foundation

Alan Wentz, Group Manager for Conservation Programs, Ducks Unlimited, Inc.

Mark Elsbree (Alternate), Vice President, Northwest Region, The Conservation Fund

Michael Dennis (Ex Officio), Vice President and General Counsel, The Nature Conservancy

Virginia Poter (Ex Officio), Director General, Canadian Wildlife Service

Martin Vargas Prieto (Ex Officio), Director, Dirección General de Vida Silvestre, SEMARNAT

Mike Johnson (Council Coordinator), Chief, Division of Bird Habitat Conservation,
U.S. Fish and Wildlife Service

recommends projects for funding approval to
The Migratory Bird Conservation Commission

Honorable Dirk Kempthorne (Chair), Secretary of the Interior

Honorable Thad Cochran, Senator from Mississippi

Honorable Blanche Lincoln, Senator from Arkansas

Honorable John Dingell, Representative from Michigan

Honorable Wayne Gilchrest, Representative from Maryland

Honorable Ed Schafer, Secretary of Agriculture

Honorable Stephen Johnson, Administrator, Environmental Protection Agency

Eric Alvarez (Secretary), Chief, Division of Realty,
U.S. Fish and Wildlife Service

The names listed above reflect current membership.

NORTH AMERICAN WETLANDS CONSERVATION ACT

Conserving North American wetland ecosystems and associated habitats for the long-term benefit of waterfowl and other wetland-associated migratory birds, fish, and wildlife.

North American Wetlands Conservation Council

NORTH AMERICAN WETLANDS CONSERVATION
COUNCIL
4401 N. FAIRFAX DRIVE, MAILSTOP 4075
ARLINGTON, VIRGINIA 22203
PH: 703-358-1784

Printed on recycled paper